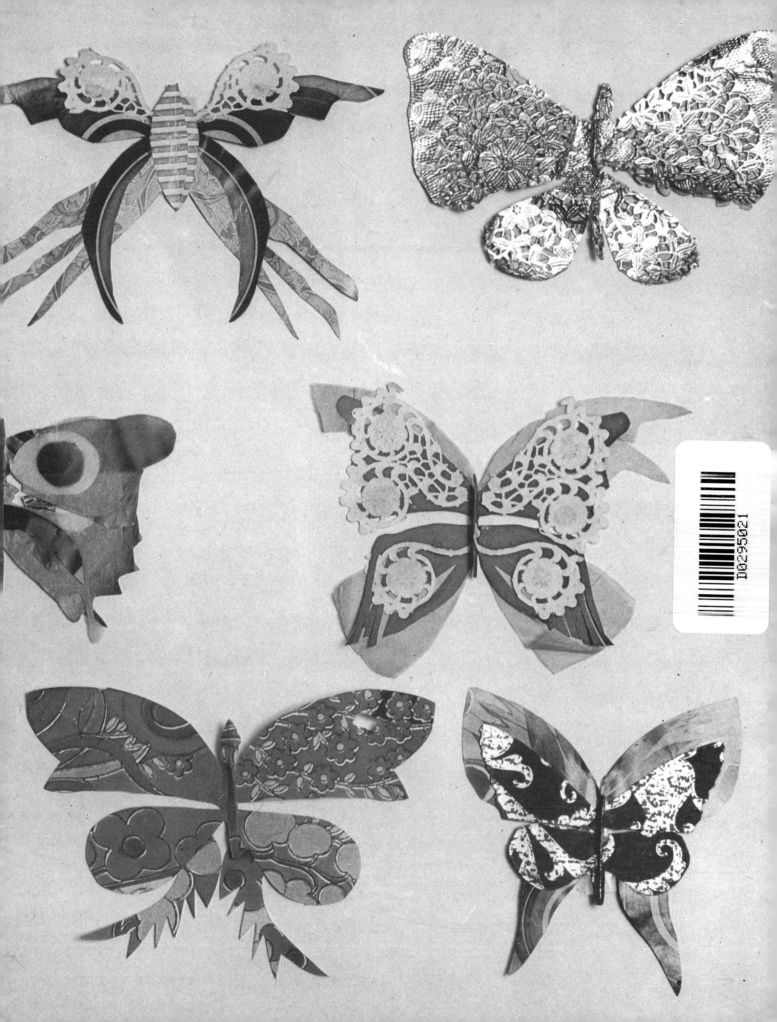

First published in Great Britain in 1978 by
Macdonald and Jane's Publishers Limited,
Paulton House,
8 Shepherdess Walk,
London N.1.
Photographs copyright © Macdonald and Jane's 1978

Made and printed in Great Britain by
Purnell & Sons Ltd, Paulton, Bristol

ISBN 0 354 08043 1

THE BIG IDEAS BOOK

SUSAN STRANKS

Photography: Peter Tebbitt
Design: Paul Chevannes

Macdonald and Jane's · London

Contents:

Have you ever wondered what to do next? That's what this book is for – to give you lots of good ideas for things to do, to make and to collect.
Most are quick and very easy, some take longer and a little more patience. I've tried them all, either on television or at home with my friends – we had our failures but mostly a terrific time. I hope you will too!

Sometimes it is easier to copy what someone is doing by **looking over their shoulder,** so please, if you're getting in a muddle with tricky things like the elephant, the dart and the star, just turn the book upside down for an over-the-shoulder view – or, of course, you can always stand on your head!

Before you start, check through the pictures of what you are going to make, and collect all the things you will need – scissors, glue, string, paper etc.
Of course you can always do the decorating part another time.

OK then – **here we go** – get some wool, scissors and card and start with these woolly-weirdos (opposite). The instructions are on page 8.

WOOLLY-BALLS

When you can make woolly-balls you will be surprised where it leads!

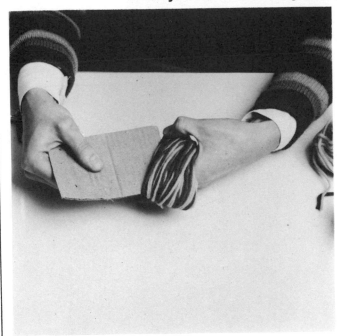

1. Wind coloured wool round a piece of card – make it really thick. Slide it off.

2. Tie firmly round the middle, twice for safety.

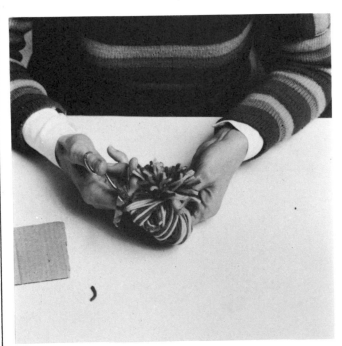

3. Cut through all the loops – you may have to trim it a bit to make it look really round.

4. Use for hats, scarves and pom-pom people – there's a weird selection one page back!

NOW SOME WOOLLY-DOLLS

1. Wind two lots of wool round a piece of card. Tie one up at the top with a small piece of wool.

2. Slide wool hanks off and thread one through the other with the knot at the top.

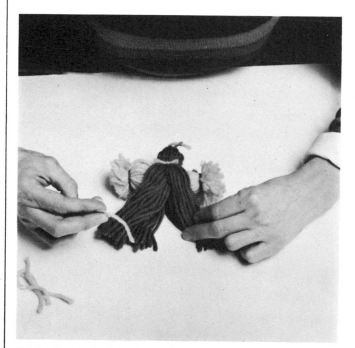

3. Tie firmly in the place shown to make the head.

4. Tie arms and separate legs. Trim ends. Sew in face.

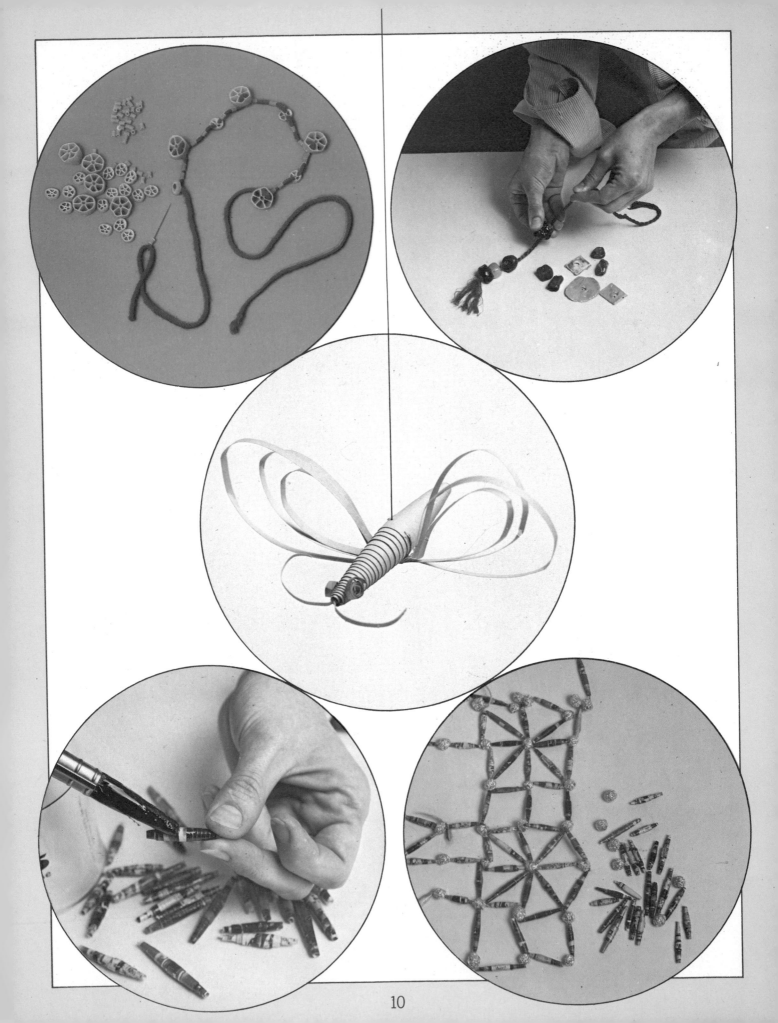

MACARONI AND STRAW BEADS

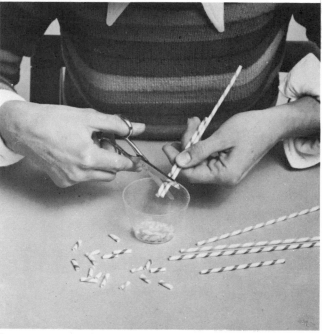

Cheap 'n' cheerful: paint pasta shapes to make beads. Home-made clay beads are fun too.

Cut up straws for beads too, into a small pot to stop them flying about.

PAPER BEADS

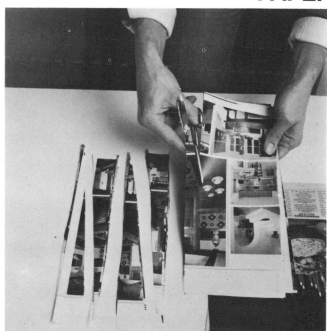

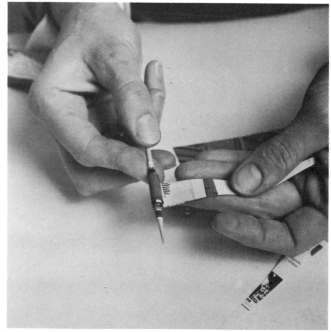

1. Take brightly coloured pages from shiny magazines – or newspapers will do. Cut them up into long triangles.

2. Roll the triangles, fat end first, round a thin knitting needle.

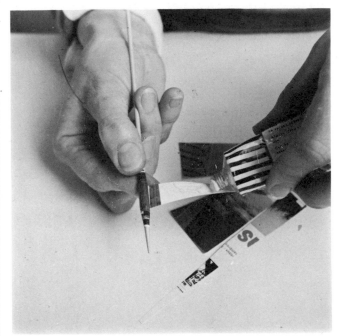

3. Put a dab of glue on the point and stick down.

4. Slide off the beads.

5. They look better if you paint them with clear shiny varnish.

6. Thread them together with rolled foil beads to make necklaces, wall hangings, bead curtains etc.

WHIRLING WHIZZERS

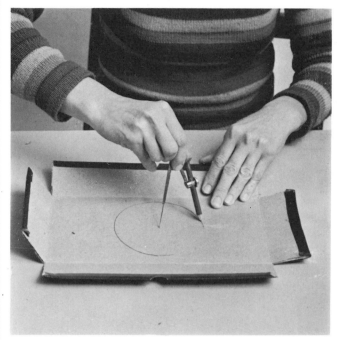

1. Use a pair of compasses to make a cardboard circle, cut out and decorate it.

2. Thread a long loop of string through two holes each side of the centre. Holding each end, spin away from you until the string is all twisted up, then gently pull the string out and in to make your whizzer spin. **(You can do the same with buttons.)**

TWIRLING TOPS

1. Make some tops out of circles of card with pencils or matches through the centre. Decorate them with paint, glitter or sequins.

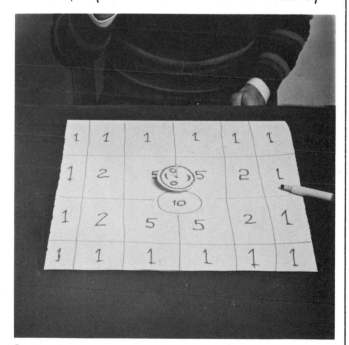

A game

2. Draw a grid with numbers on it. Flick your top in the air to land on the grid and keep spinning. Whichever number it stops at adds to your score.

LANTERNS

These are really easy to make and very effective too

Fold a long sheet of paper in half. Cut a deep fringe on the folded edge. Open and bend round and stick the two ends together. Make a paper strip for the handle and hang it up.

Add paint and glitter for Christmas.

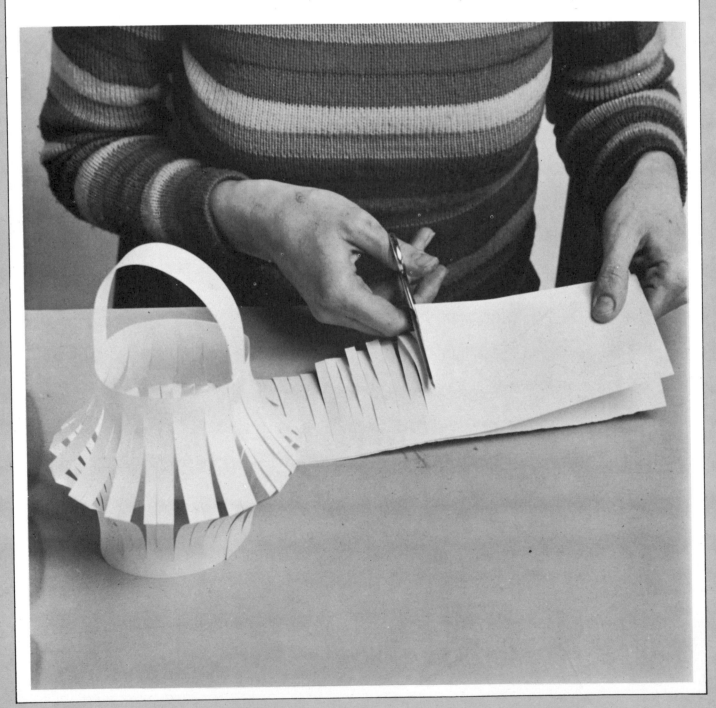

PAPER HOUSES

A Danish friend showed me an easy way to make paper houses — here's how!

1. Take a sheet of paper.

2. Fold in half longways.

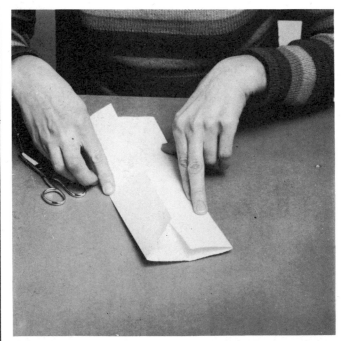

3. Open out again and fold both outside edges to the middle.

4. Now also bend in both the top and bottom ends – these folds should each measure the same as one of the longways ones.

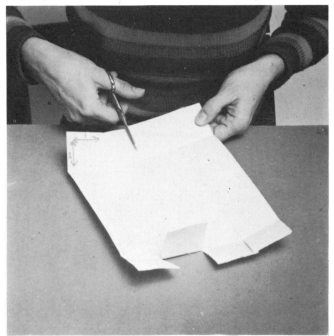

5. Cut tabs lengthways as far as the crossways folds.

6. Turn over. Fold and stick ends.

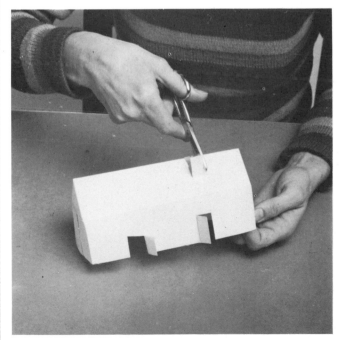

7. Cut doors and chimneys.

Make them very big out of stiffer paper if you want to decorate your houses, and try making a village round a silver-foil pond with paper ducks and trees.

I like to decorate mine when they are standing up, but you can do yours flat.

WIGWAMS

Wigwams or tepees are traditional American Indian homes – make some out of coloured paper.

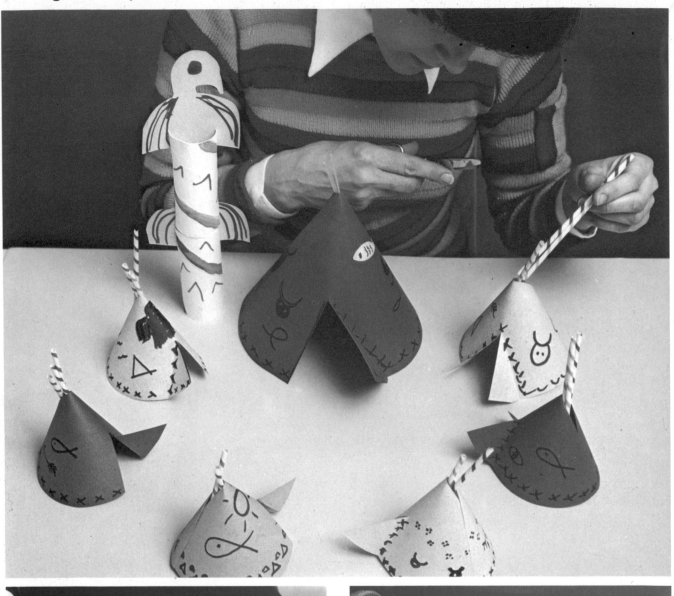

1. Take several sheets of paper and pile them together – draw a circle on the top one.

2. Cut out circles all together and fold in half. Open again.

18

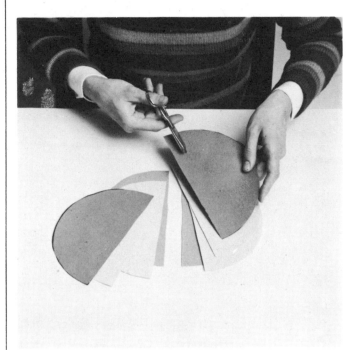

3. Cut in half down the centre fold.

4. Decorate while flat – cut an opening. Spread glue along cut edge.

5. Bend round and stick cut edge to itself. Make lots and a big one for the chief!

6. Make a totem pole, an Indian baby cradle and other things for your village.

Decorations should be arrows, bows, crosses, eagles, canoes etc.
Look in books to find other traditional Indian symbols for your wigwams.

PAPER LINKS

This pretty paper linking is well worth learning. If you have patience you can make a wall-hanging or a window blind out of different coloured chains on a pole.

1. Cut out lots of paper oblongs (about postcard size). Fold in half lengthways.

2. And in half crossways. (Like a hanky.)

3. Draw this half 'stirrup' shape with the narrow bit on the folded corner (where I am holding it). Cut out. Use the first shape as a pattern for the others.

4. Open out the shapes and link them through each other.

USE LEATHER OR FELT
TO MAKE A BELT!

PAPER ROLLS
Paper Rolls are useful for making all sorts of things

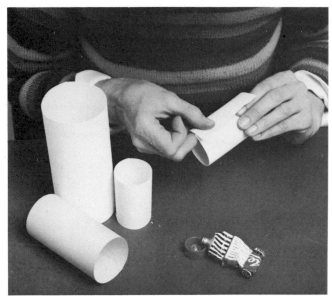

Cut strips of stiff paper in different widths and lengths and glue the ends together.

Use for making animals, turrets of castles, bodies of lorries, oil tankers, lighthouses and so on.
Don't forget you can use cardboard rolls from toilet rolls and kitchen paper as well.

This is **Smudge.**
His legs and head are **squashed** paper rolls of different sizes.

How many times does **Smudge** appear in this book? Answer on page 140.

BUNNY RABBITS

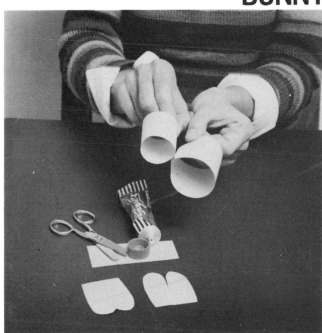

1. Make two paper rolls (one a bit smaller than the other) and stick them together.

2. Add paper ears and feet and a fluffy cotton-wool tail. Draw a face and whiskers.

Rabbits breed quickly – so now make a family!

OWL

Make a paper roll (or use a cardboard one). Stick it closed at one end – cut out a curved bit. May be better to cut out first, then stick. Add big round eyes, a beak and claws.

Look whooo whooo you've got!

CAT 'N' FISH

Make the cat's head like the owl's but with catty eyes and face. Cut out a flat body with four legs, wider at the back, and curl it over. Add a tail and a fish or two.

And that's mihow to make a cat.

STARS

Know how to cut out a star? It's easy. You can use **any** shaped piece of paper – but I used a square because it was easier to show with.

1. Take a piece of paper.

2. Fold in half.

3. Fold in half again the other way.

4. Fold the folded point in half again. Keep the point towards you.

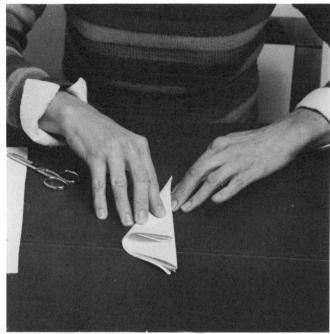

5. Fold the point in half again. Keep the point towards you.

6. Now cut off the point on the slant.

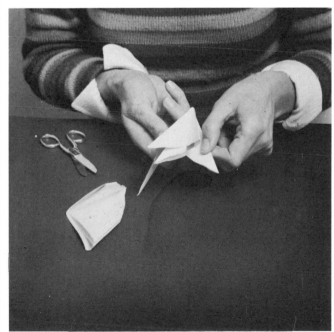

7. Open up and there's your star!

8. Once you have got the knack – make more stars by chopping more and more off the point before you unfold it. Cover with glitter and hang them up on different lengths of cotton for a Christmas mobile.

PAINTED WOODEN THINGS

Now and again everyone gets the urge to paint on something other than paper. Why not start with wooden spoons? They are cheap and easy to find, and make original presents. Some spoons are waxy or rough and need a rub with fine sandpaper before you start.

1. Paint your spoon with poster colour and let it dry.

2. Paint any pattern you want – daisies and dots are easy! Let it dry.

3. You can get a really professional finish with two coats of glossy transparent varnish; let one dry before the next one goes on.

4. Try other things: brushes, mops, flower pots, even a wooden chair.

WAYS WITH CARDBOARD BOXES

Big cardboard boxes from grocers or drink-stores are marvellous for all sorts of things. Here are some ideas. I haven't decorated these – but of course you can paint or paper them as you wish. Use a small saw or an old bread knife to cut.
You may need help.

Filing tray for keeping comics and magazines in. Cut a shallow box diagonally – insert sheets of card with reference numbers or letters on the outside edge.

Theatre
Open box front and leave the two back flaps for bracing. Cut a long slot in the top for scenery and holes in the sides or bottom for glove or stick puppets.

A party game
Take a bottle box – leave in the divisions.
Label each hole with a number.
Try and throw a cork or a ball into the hole with the highest number for the highest score and best prize.

This is good for a charity fete too.

Decorate your theatre and add curtains.

Chair
1. Draw slanting guide lines on each side of the box from bottom centre to top edge (3 cms from end). Measure so they are both the same.

2. Saw down the lines to the bottom edge, carefully.

3. Open out.

4. There's your chair!
Use plenty of strong sticky tape and more cardboard to reinforce it.

PAINT – OR COVER WITH PATTERNED PAPER OR FABRIC.

QUICK CHICKS

Want to make a hasty chick?
You can do it in a tick.
Take a cotton ball or two
Sequin eyes, a dab of glue.
Wash an empty egg shell clean
Make a beak – see what I mean?
Stick the lot together, quick
There – you've got your hasty chick!

WHAT HAS A PAPER WEIGHT TO DO WITH A BROKEN LEG?

Plaster of paris… is a finely powdered plaster, which, when mixed with water, sets very fast. It is often used with gauze bandages to make casts for broken limbs. Buy a bag at your nearest large dispensing chemist.

1. Put some water in a jug or bowl – add the plaster to it. Not too much at first; stir well – it should be a thick, creamy consistency.

2. Dust your moulds with a little dry plaster. Pour the liquid plaster into them – saucers, bowls, paper cake-cups to make fake cakes (leave them double for strength).

3. When it starts to set, which is right away, push a wire loop into the mixture if it is to be a wall plaque and hold for a minute or two.

4. Leave moulds for a good hour, or longer if you are using a deep mould. Tap or squeeze the vessel to loosen the plaster object… and there it is! We put a coin in the bottom of our saucer for fun.

PAPER WEIGHTS AND WALL PLAQUES

5. For a hand use a rubber glove. Peg the glove firmly on a line, or hold it until the plaster is set. It goes warm while it's setting!

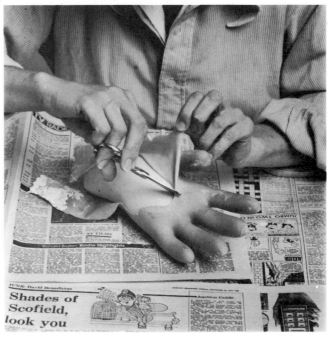

6. You have to cut off the glove, or the fingers will break.

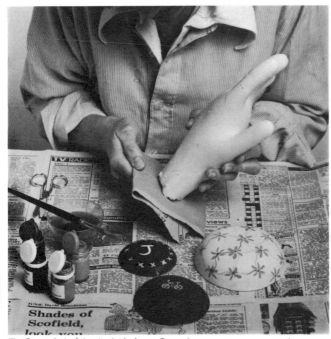

7. Careful, it's brittle!... Sandpaper any roughness, and paint it if you want to.

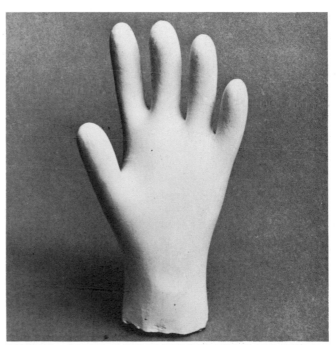

BEWARE... COVER EVERYTHING INCLUDING YOURSELF... IT'S MESSY! ONLY USE OLD BOWLS AND JUGS FOR THIS AND HAVE A BUCKET OF WATER STANDING BY TO SOAK THEM IN.

Important: you must work quickly as the plaster sets fast, and soak all your tools and bowls immediately in cold water to get them clean.

CANDLE HOLDER

Use any shaped container – a milk carton is good. To make holes put in your candles and waggle them about a bit as the plaster is drying or they'll stick fast!

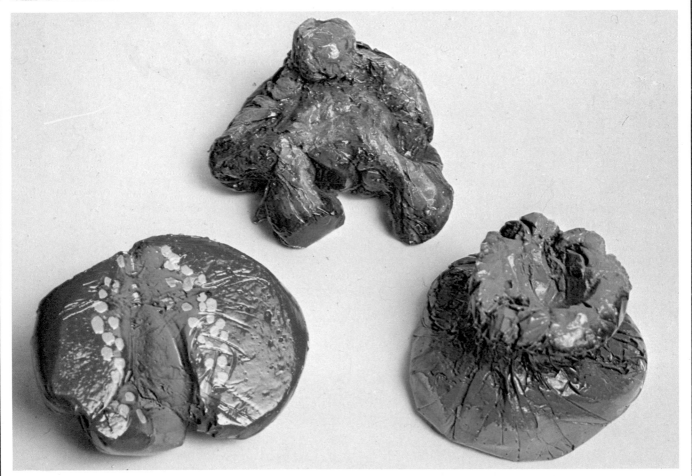

GLUMPS

Pour wet plaster into polythene bags. As it dries, squash into funny shapes. When hard, peel off bags and paint. I thought this grey one was just like an old seated man.

Your painted plaster things look best with two coats of shiny clear varnish.

CUT OUT SHAPES

1. Many shapes—hearts, butterflies, triangles, clubs, diamonds, circles and such are so easy to cut out if you just fold the paper and cut on the fold.

2. To make lots at once just use several sheets folded together.

PAPER BUTTERFLIES

1. Fold several sheets of paper in half. On the folded edge draw half butterflies of different shapes – cut them out.

2. Decorate with paint, glitter, sequins or stickers. Hang up on cotton in your window to waft in the breeze or stick on straws or sticks and 'plant' in pots.

VALENTINE LOVE HEART

1. Cut out two tiny paper hearts the same size. Stick centre folds together along a strand of cotton (use very little glue).

2. Dangle it above your open palm. It will spin round.
Clockwise he/she loves you
Anti-clockwise he/she loves you not.

STAND UP SHAPES

SEE-THROUGH PATTERNS

Make stand up shapes by cutting a slit to halfway along your shapes. Slot them together. Try it with other shapes including figures and Christmas trees.

Fold up thin paper lots of times (tissue is best). Trim out tiny, different-shaped holes. Open up for a nice surprise!
Try sticking one colour over another to make greetings cards (tiny dabs of glue). Turn over to see how lovely they look in colour....

I don't like sending ordinary cards for birthdays and things—do you? It's fun to make your own and quick too. Here are some more ideas you may not have thought of.

Try stencilling – spray paint through cut-out shapes and over various objects using a small brush or a can of spray paint.

Tear tissue paper shapes and stick them down lightly.

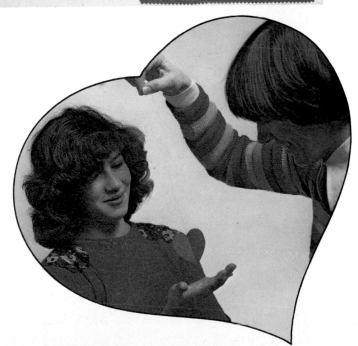

A NEEDLE CASE

I always hate throwing away small diaries when next year comes round. They have such smart covers and are often real leather. Here's something you can use them for.

1. Tear out the old insides.

2. Stick a piece of patterned fabric or paper over the rough bits.

3. Now cut several smaller layers of felt (other material will do) and lay them across.

4. Sew them firmly in through to the back of the cover.

5. Don't forget to disguise the word 'Diary' with a small label saying **'Needles'** or **'Happy Birthday'** or even a name.

1. Bend an oblong piece of cardboard in half down the middle (the corrugated kind is best). Cover the outside by glueing on fabric or wrapping paper. Keep bending it while you glue or it won't close!

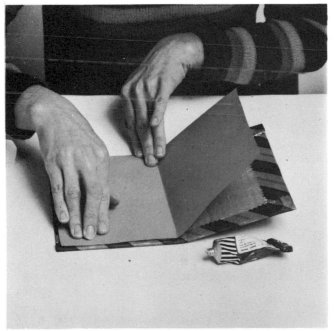

2. Cover the inside too – I used plain paper for mine.

3. Stick two paper pockets across the bottom to hold the writing paper and envelopes.

A ROMAN MOSAIC

Choose a favourite picture, or draw and paint one. Cut it into tiny squares and stick it on a larger piece of coloured card. **Do a strip at a time** or you will muddle up the pieces dreadfully!

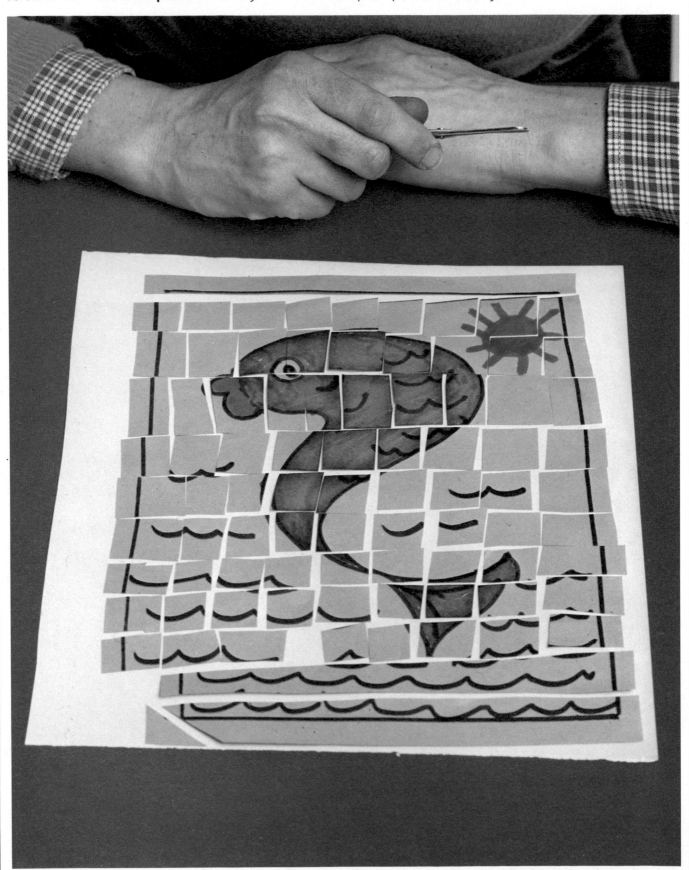

AN ARAB BELT
You need two of you to do this because it is so long. (See previous page.)

Take three bunches of wool with at least twelve strands in each (they must be long enough to go round your waist four times).

1. Bind strands together a quarter of the way in from one end and start plaiting (roll into balls for easy handling).

2. Bind your plait a quarter of the way from the other end – bend in half and bind into a loop. Start two smaller plaits each end and, after a bit, bind them.

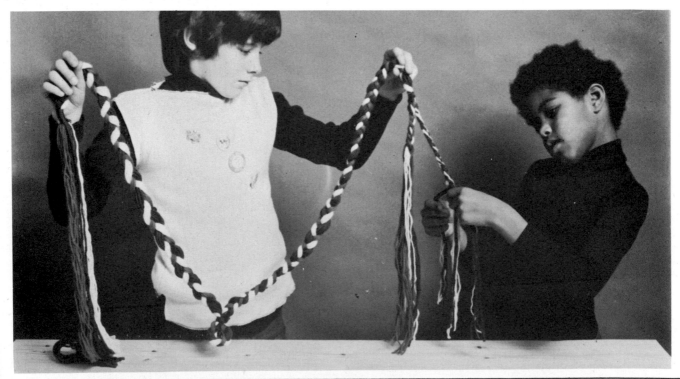

3. Now separate the end strands and finish with tinier plaits (three or four each end) and tinkling bells from a pet shop (or two curtain rings tied together will do). Bind in one large and two small woolly balls at the junctions (see page 8).

This does take a long time and you may need to change the position of the big ball to get the size just right.

FABULOUS PAPER FLOWERS

Make up your own variations.
I even use newspaper and doilies. Try sticking wrapped sweets in the centre of some of your flowers.

1. Fold several sheets of coloured tissue paper in half.

2. And in half the other way (like a hanky).

3. Fold again on the folded corner to make a point.

4. Cut a curved petal shape opposite the folded point.

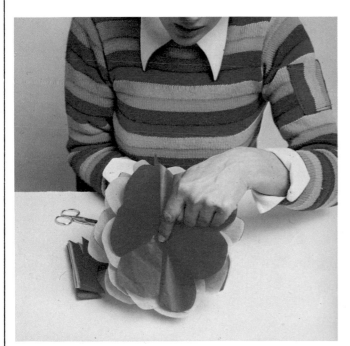

5. Open out and push a finger into the centre.

6. Tie round the back with sticky tape (wool or flower wire) and stick on a branch from the garden.

FIESTA MASKS

1. Make some 'papier maché' by tearing small pieces of newspaper into paste (wallpaper paste or flour mixed with water). Squash it all to a mash.

2. Blow up a balloon and cover it all over with the flat soaked pieces. Do three or four layers. Leave in warm place to dry and stiffen.

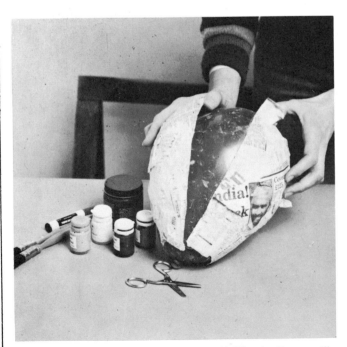

3. When it is dry, cut carefully in half. The balloon will probably go pop; mine didn't!
Cut eye holes and decorate the masks.

You can make good stick masks using paper plates.

Here are two ideas – they look great covered in foil too.

A LITTLE MAGIC

Bet I can get through this postcard!...
Toby thought it was nonsense
so I showed him.

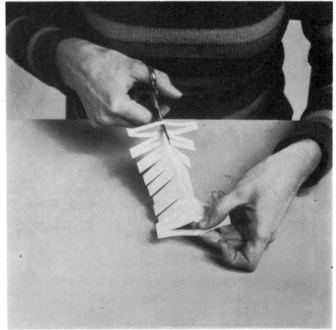

1. Fold postcard in half. Starting on the folded edge cut backwards and forwards along it. Your last cut should start on the folded edge too, but don't cut right across.

2. Open up card and cut along the centre fold – like this. But don't cut through the strips at each end.

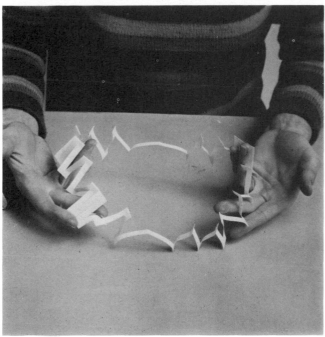

3. Open out gently.

4. See – I got through it easily, so did Toby and I won my bet!

NEWSPAPER FUN – DANCING DOLLS

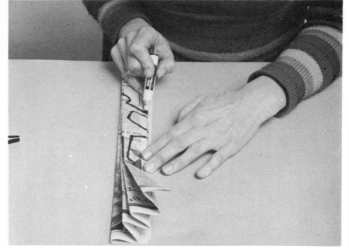

1. Fold a sheet of newspaper back and forth like a concertina.

2. Draw half a doll on the folded edge. Make sure the arms and skirt reach the opposite edge.

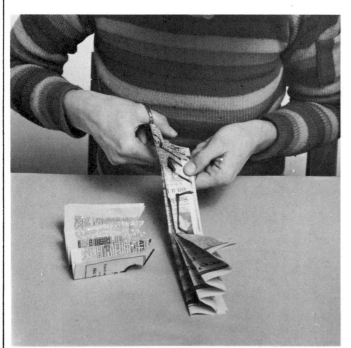

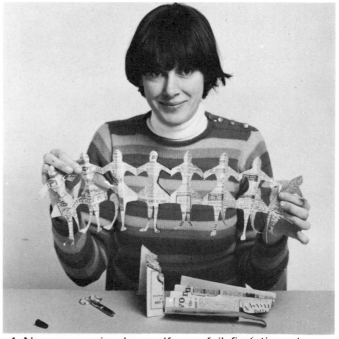

3. Cut out – except where the arms and skirt touch the edge. Open out.

4. Newspaper is cheap. If you fail first time, have another go!

Try rabbits and other things too.

NEWSPAPER FUN – RAZZLE DAZZLE TREE

1. Take several separate sheets of newspaper.

2. Roll up, but not too tight.

3. Hold the top together firmly and tear some strips to halfway down.

4. Grab an inside bit of the roll and pull up gently, twisting a little.

A MAGIC BOX

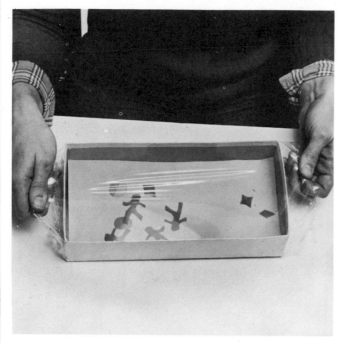

1. Cut out some small figures and shapes from thin paper (tissue is best) and put them in a shallow box.

2. Cover the top with cling film (stretch it tight and smooth).

3. Rub the top fast with your finger-tips – keep going and the figures will dance about.

Ask your friends if they know why . . . Answer on page 140. Make a pocket version with a match box.

BALANCING TRICK

Take a cork, push two forks into it and a pin in the bottom. If you are careful you can now balance the head of the pin on the edge of a bottle.

Do you know what the prongs of a fork are really called? Answer page 140.

MAGIC PICTURES

1. Draw a picture with a piece of wax candle.

2. Spread paint over it and there's your secret picture.

YES-NO BOX

It will answer all your secret questions.

1. Slide out the tray from a match-box and draw this two-way face on the back and front of it. (I have used two boxes to show you how.) Slide back the tray.

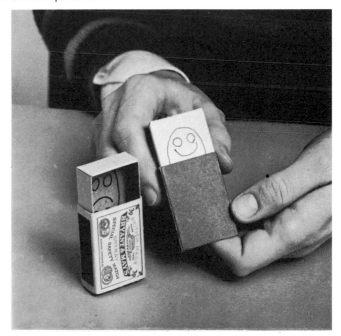

2. Whisper a secret question needing a 'yes' or 'no' answer into your box, close it again. Toss the box into the air and it will fall angled towards you. Pick it up as it has fallen and open it up slowly. The face gives the answer!

Now try it on your friends.

DECORATIVE BALLS

These light and lovely hanging balls are made from round lumps of polystyrene stuck with paper flowers and Christmas-tree balls.

Make the flowers from tissue or crêpe-paper (pages 46–47). Wind the backs with flower-wire or hair-pins and stick in the polystyrene. You can use a ball of chicken-wire for the base if you prefer but mind your hands.

Try other shapes too – diamonds and triangles for instance. Polystyrene can be saved from boxes and packing cases. Use a sharp knife or scissors to trim it carefully to the shape you want, but it often comes in good and interesting shapes anyway.

SWEET SMELLING PRESENTS... HERB BAGS

1. Cut out circles of fabrics (old tights will do).

2. Put some sweet herbs in the circles. You can use pads of perfumed cotton wool if you have no herbs.

3. Tie them into bags with ribbon-bows. Decorate them if you like.

...POMANDERS

POMANDERS

In the old days when houses didn't have running water, drains were pretty bad and people didn't wash much. So they made pomanders to carry about under their noses and hide the nasty smells.

1. Take an orange and divide it into quarters with sticky-tape.
Make holes with a fork first. **Don't put your hand underneath**, you may hurt it. Stick each quarter with cloves very close together.

2. Dry it on a radiator or in an airing cupboard until hard. Remove tape and decorate it with pretty tape and ribbon.

Wrong way

Right way

ORANGE PEEL TEETH

Make these beastly teeth from wide strips of orange peel – wash the orange first!

Make the grown-ups try them too; they look monstrous.

Pretend to be the person you look like, change your voice. You will feel quite different and the things you say will surprise you.

HANDBAG

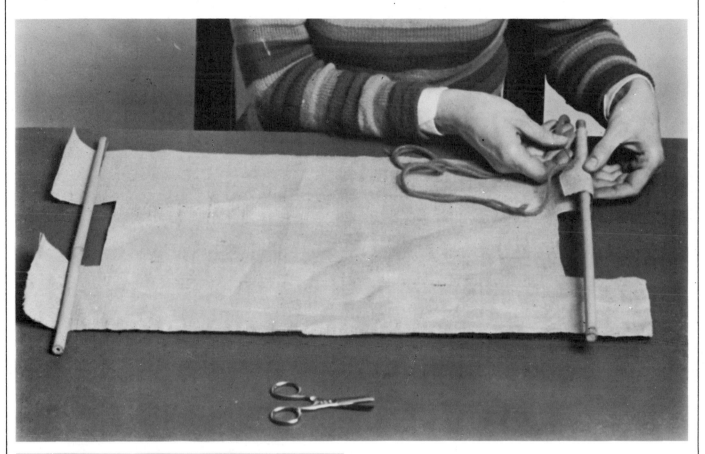

Cut out this shape of material and sew the ends round two straight sticks. Hessian on cane sticks looks nice.

Stick or, if it's for heavy things, sew up the sides and decorate with a fabric picture or embroidery.

A LUCKY BLACK CAT

1. Draw and cut out two shapes like these from black paper (change the body a bit if you like).

2. Stick the inside end of the tail to the bottom of the cat. Hang up on cotton.

SHADOW PORTRAITS

1. Stick up a sheet of white paper. Sit someone in a chair in front of it and place a bright light so that their profile-shadow is on the paper. Draw round their head and face as close as you can – whoops, I've gone a bit wrong! The subject must sit very still.

2. Fill in the outline with dark paint.

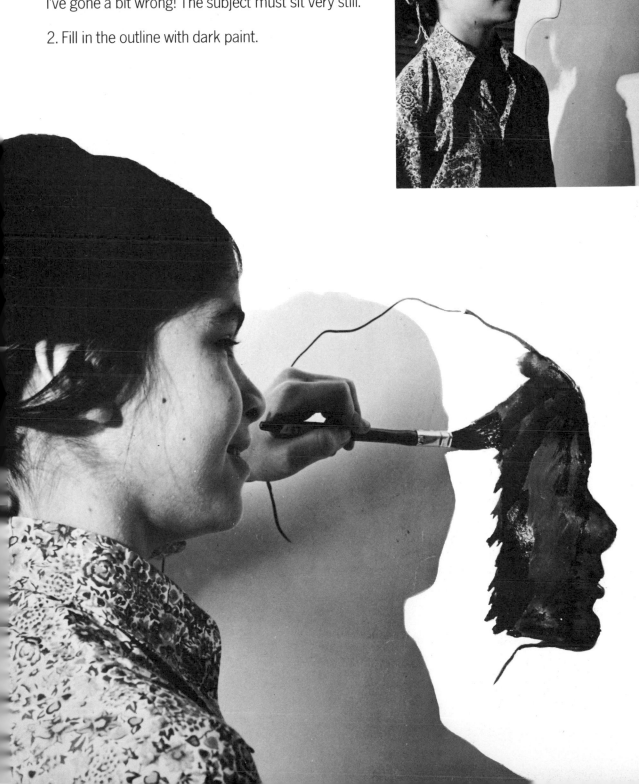

PAPER DART

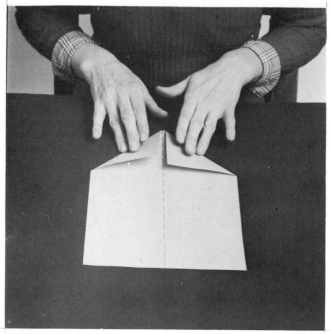

1. Take an oblong sheet of paper. Fold two corners down to the middle.

2. Fold in half with corners inside.

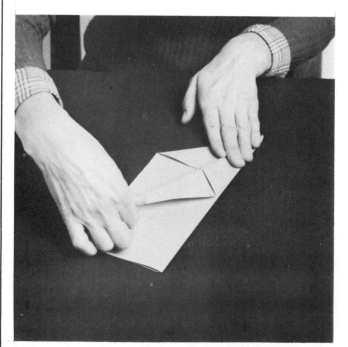

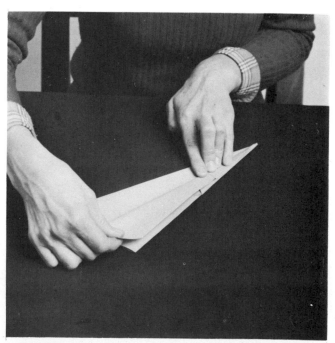

3. Turn one folded corner out to line up with the centre fold – now do the other.

4. Fold the two wings in half again to line up with the centre fold.

5. Now your dart is ready to fly.

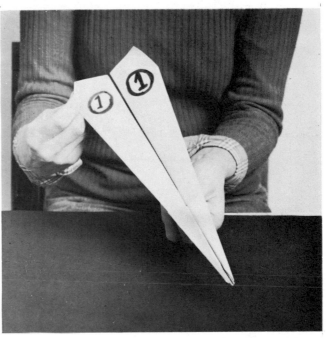

6. Make all your folds very sharp. You can bend up the wings for better flight.

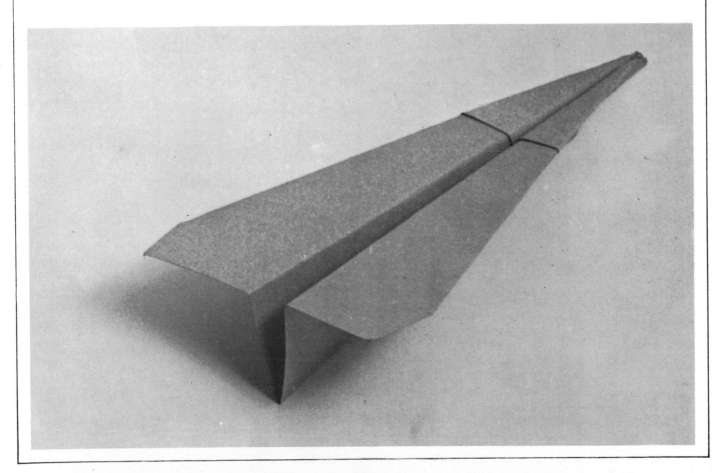

1.
Celery
Apple
Spring onion
Nuts
Raisins and
Dressing Number 2

2.
Grated carrot
Mandarin oranges (tinned)
and Dressing Number 1
(add orange juice)

3.
Mushrooms
Peppers (capsicums)
Spring (or round) onions
and Dressing Number 1

Avocado pears
and peppers usually
cost a lot, but are
worth trying on
special occasions.

Dressing
number 1:
¾ oil, ¼ vinegar –
salt – pepper –
mustard
number 2:
As above plus a
dollop of mayonnaise
(mix well)

SIX SCRUMPTIOUS SALADS
**Try out some new side-salads on your friends and family –
add meat, fish or cheese for starters or main courses.**

4.
Frankfurters
Hard boiled egg
Cress (or water cress)
Avocado pear
and Dressing Number 1
(add mixed herbs)

5.
Red beans (tinned)
Cucumber
Onion
Peppers (capsicums)
and Dressing Number 1
(add a little honey)

6.
Tuna fish
Sweetcorn
Avocado pear
Tomatoes
and Dressing Number 2
(add chopped onion)

Now make up your
own – here are
more things to try:

Raw cabbage
Raw cauliflower
Beetroot
Cooked green beans
and peas
Cheese
Cooked meat
and sausages
Crispy bacon
Radishes
*Potatoes and onions and
dressing number 2 make potato salad.

PRINTING
Spread newspaper.

1. In a tray of kitchen foil put layers of paper kitchen towel or tissues. Wet thoroughly.

2. Dab on plenty of ink or paint.

3. Try printing patterns with potatoes.

4. Apples.

Now try other things – corks, plasticine shapes, your own hands, fingers and feet but **not on a carpet** and have someone by you to wash your feet!
Make your own wrapping paper or even wallpaper.

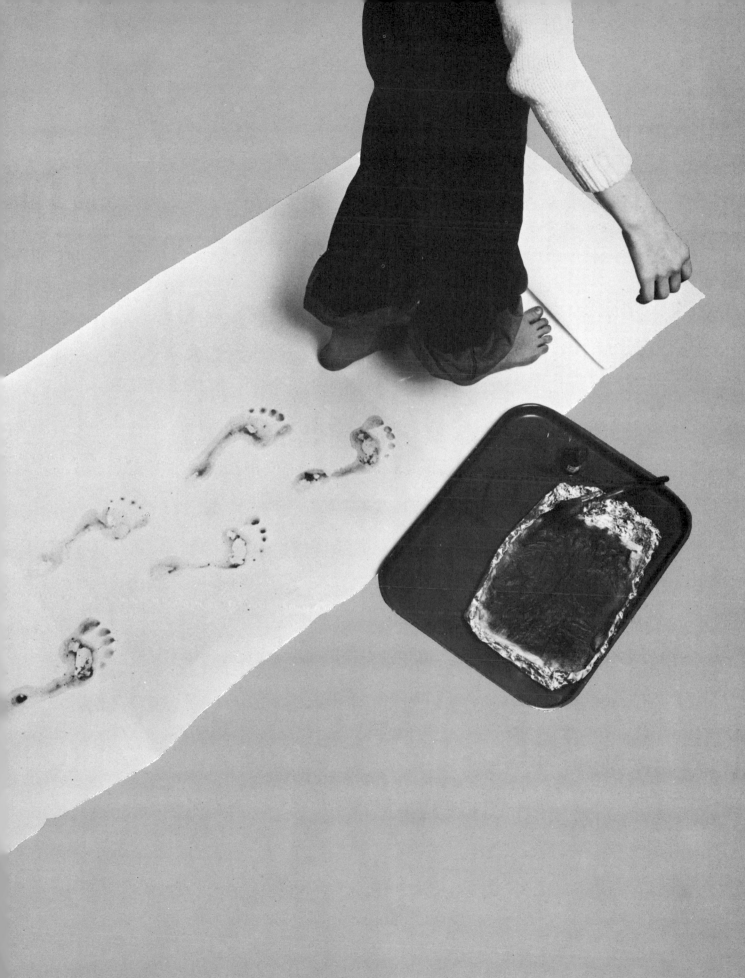

TO MAKE A PIECE OF PAPER SQUARE

This is very important for making certain things.

1. Just fold one corner of a sheet of paper across to the other side.

2. Press down fold, keeping the edges together.

3. Cut off the spare piece along the straight edge.

4. Open out and there's a square.

HOW ABOUT A WINDMILL ?

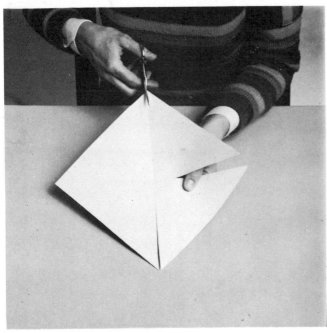

1. Take a **square** sheet of paper. Fold both ways corner to corner. Open up. Cut in from the four corners along the folds nearly to the centre.

2. Push a pin through a tiny square of card. Then slide every other corner up on to the pin. You may make a 'bosh' of it the first time but just copy the picture and try again.

3. Push the pin through the back and turn over. Thread a small button or bead on to the pin and push into a cork – **mind** your finger with the pin head!

4. Push a pointed stick or a pencil into the cork and decorate the windmill. It will spin as you run with it, or move it forwards and backwards.

AN UNUSUAL ELEPHANT

The Japanese have always been masters of the art of paper-folding; their word for it is ORIGAMI, and many of the complicated designs take ages to perfect. They seem to like making animals; try this Origami elephant. . .

1. Take a **square** sheet of paper. (See how on page 68) Fold in half corner to corner and open out again.

2. Fold two corners in and down to centre fold.

3. Close over centre fold again.

4. Bend sharp corner back across the centre fold and press down.

5. A bit tricky this – open out head with two fingers.

6. Bend open head double.

7. Draw on two eyes and you will see your elephant. Bend the face in half around to the front.

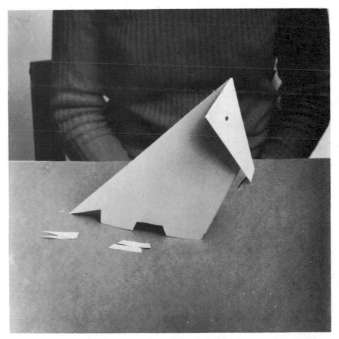

8. Bend down the trunk and trim the base to make feet and tail shape.

* Always make your folds very sharp.

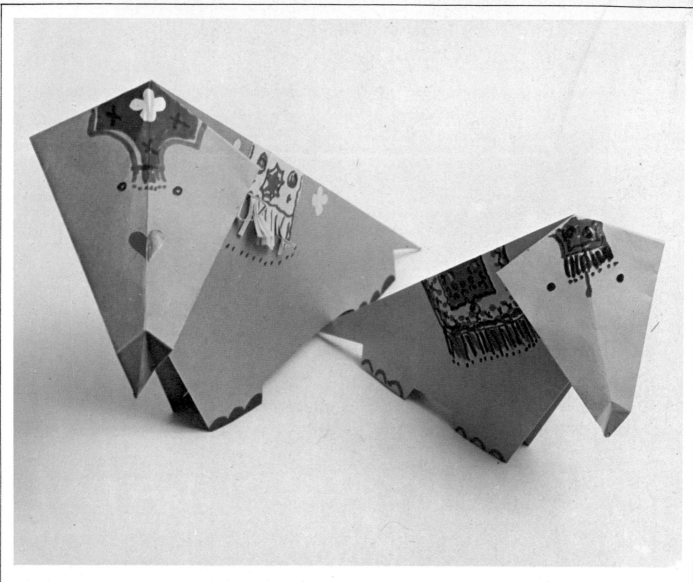

Fold two paper strips together 'concertina style' and make a dragon.

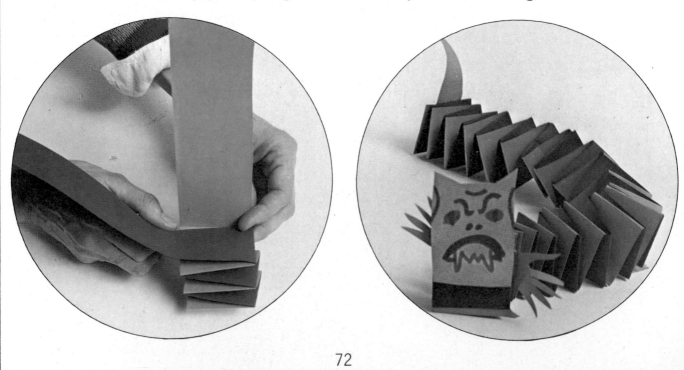

72

1

2

3

4

5

6

7

TRY TIE-DYE

Buy some cold water dyes and brighten up your T-shirts, skirts, jeans and scarves. Follow the instructions to mix the dye. **You may need help.** Use a large sink or bowl so the fabric can move about easily.

You can make marvellous patterns like marbling, circles, sunbursts and zigzags by tying up your fabric first. Guess which of these makes the patterns on the previous page. Answers on page 140.

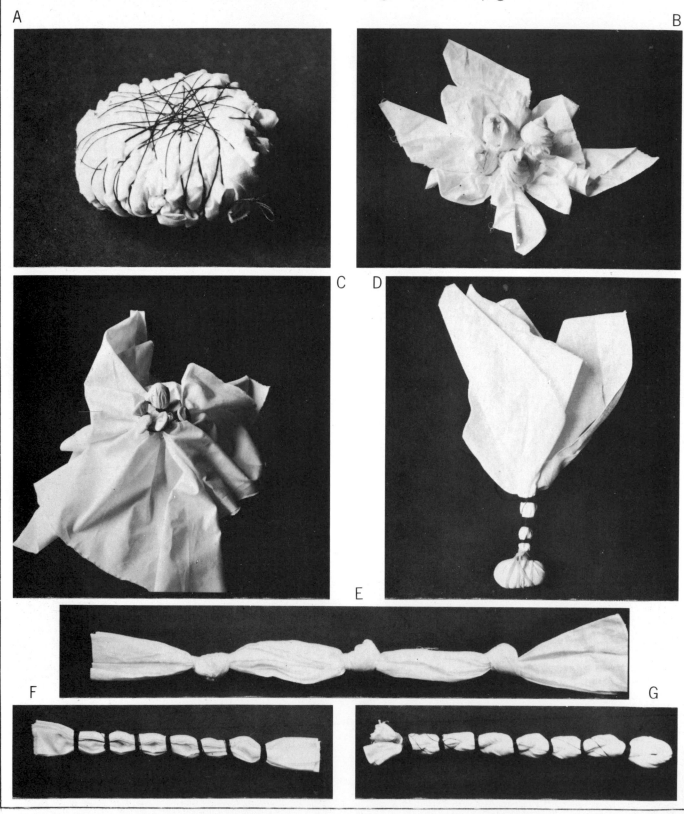

PAINT YOUR OWN T-SHIRT

Why not buy some fabric paint from an art shop and paint a design on a plain T-shirt? Start with something simple the first time – a star or a butterfly for instance. If you are nervous, practise on a scrap of fabric first.

1. Slide a piece of cardboard into the T-shirt to keep the design off the back.

2. Draw a simple picture – or use a stencil like Alison's butterfly. Stick the shirt and the stencil down with sticky tape. Dab fabric paint on well with a cotton-wool pad or paint with a brush.

3. Careful how you lift the stencil – don't smudge it!

Finish according to instructions on pot – most fabric paints need ironing on the wrong side of the fabric to set.

PARACHUTES

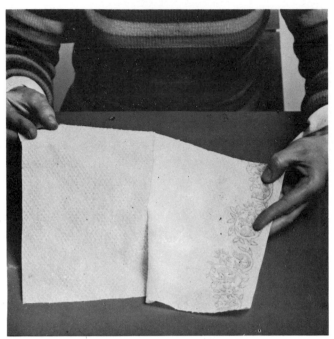

1. Separate tissues or kitchen paper.

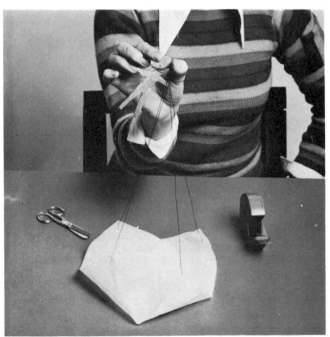

2. Stick four cotton strands all the same length to the corners and join the free ends to the head of a cork, or a small cardboard figure.

3. Throw them up and watch them float to earth.

EGG BOX DECORATIONS

1. How many different decorations can you make from an old egg box?

2. I tried spirals and flowers and bells with foil balls in them.

3. You can add paint and glitter and hang them on a white painted twig.

Make a monster with an egg box head and a fat body made of papier maché over a balloon (see page 48). His legs are cardboard rolls pushed into holes in the body and covered with papier maché.

SAVE YOUR CONTAINERS

Don't forget all those empty bottles, jars or pots, especially soft plastic ones, that can be cut down to make other useful shapes.

To remove any writing or ugly patterns before decorating I use fine wire wool and a bit of hard rubbing. Use for planting . . . page 126
paper flowers . . . . pages 46 –47
wall boards . . . . . page 111

AND YOUR OLD SOCKS

Don't forget sock puppets. Just add eyes and teeth, fangs and hair to make different characters.

And you can make a cuddly mouse by chopping off the top and toe of an old sock and stuffing them into the middle bit with some extra padding (old tights perhaps). Sew closed back and front and stick on felt ears and eyes, and string whiskers and tail.

GLASS JARS

These were ordinary coffee jars – you could do the same with any empty jar or pot. Fill them with bath salts, small soaps, cotton-wool or sweets.

Look at containers and cartons carefully sometimes you can cut something out of them.

SAVE YOUR EMPTY CANS

They make good skittles for parties and charity fetes. You can always use a woolly ball for indoors. See page 8.

EGG COSIES

These make terrific Easter presents

See – my chicken nearly wasn't big enough.

Cut out some double shapes of felt which will go easily round a big egg with edges to spare.
Eggs are fatter than you think!
Stick or sew the shapes together and add trimmings.

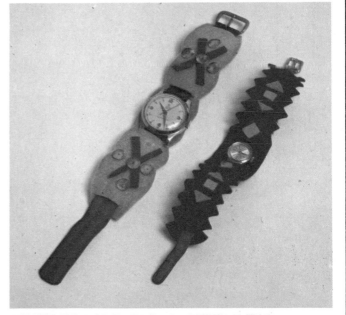

FANCY WATCH STRAPS

Decorate a wide strip of felt, cut four slits in it and thread your watch strap through each side.

GLAD RAG DOLLS

A bit more difficult – try and get someone who can sew to help!

1. Fold some thinnish fabric double and pin it to stop it slipping – draw and cut out these shapes (I used calico cotton).

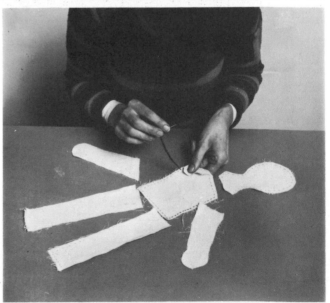

2. Sew the edges together with running stitch, leaving one end open for stuffing, and turn the sections right side out.

3. Stuff with cut rags or tights. If using kapok, work inside a polythene bag to stop it flying about.

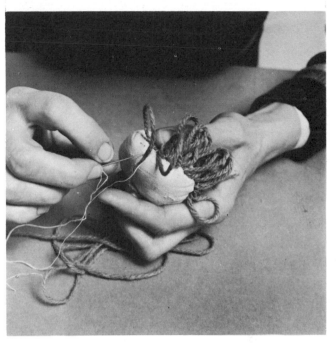

4. Sew wool hair in loops all over the head then cut for a tousled look (or you can try other styles).

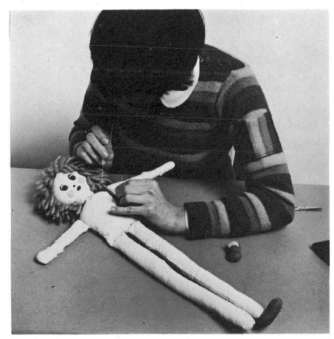

5. Close all the open ends and sew your doll together – add tiny stuffed felt feet if you want and a cheerful felt face.

6. Measure the doll and make up your own clothes from simple tubes of fabric sewn together and gathered for waists and wrists. Add lace, buttons and fancy trimmings.

I've done drawings to show you on the next page.

Basic Skirt

A wide tube of fabric gathered in round the waist with elastic or thick thread.

Basic Shirt or Blouse

Two tubes of fabric for sleeves (wide for puffed, narrow for straight). Squarish tube for body with two top slits to sew sleeves in. Gather wrists and neckline with thick thread. You can open up the front if you like to make a jacket – and add a collar too.

Make the same thing long for a nightie and tie round the middle for a dress.

Basic Trousers

Two narrow tubes of fabric, left open inside top and sewn together, gathered round waist with elastic or thick thread.

Tips

Make patterns with kitchen towelling or paper tissues first. Always pin the fabric before you sew (use fabric glue if you like).

Make your clothes inside out so the rough edges will be hidden; turn right side out for decorating with lace, ribbon, braid, buttons, etc.

SIMPLE GLOVE PUPPETS

Make these out of cardboard or paper rolls with fabric stuck on. the front. You can create any character you want using wool, buttons, extra fabric and paper, broken jewellery, sequins and so on.

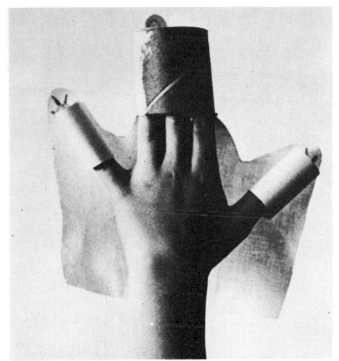

LEAF AND FLOWER PRESSING

Keep your best leaves and flowers pressed flat between the pages of an old telephone book under more HEAVY BOOKS. Put the delicate ones between tissue or blotting paper first. Don't forget where you have left them! You can use them to make lovely pictures and book marks – turn to the next page and see how.

LEAF PICTURES AND BOOK MARKS

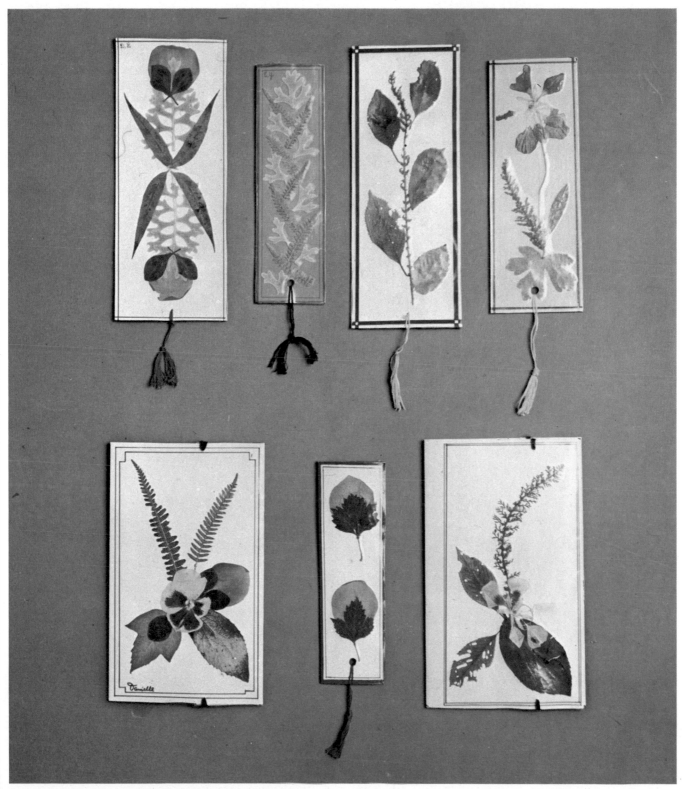

Lay out your leaves in the pattern you want before sticking them in place with tiny dabs of glue – keep the colours fresh with a coat of clear, shiny varnish.

Nature sculptures out of fir-cones, feathers and bark can be interesting too.

Lay your pressed petals and grasses on thin cards in pretty patterns. Cover smoothly with cling-film (take over edges to back) and then stick on another piece of card to cover the back. Finish off with tassels or ribbons.

COAL HOLE COVERS

Watch out for coal holes! I don't mean just to make sure you don't fall down them, but look at the covers.

Some are very interesting and beautiful relics of years ago when most houses had regular deliveries of coal for their open fires.

I was surprised to find six different examples of early cast iron coal-hole covers in my little street, so I made a collection of rubbings to hang on the wall.

Glue a stick top and bottom of the rubbing and hang it by cord or ribbon.

To make some table-mats you cover them with cling-film (cold food only). Or try them under the glass top of a coffee table.

1. First brush all the grit and dust out.

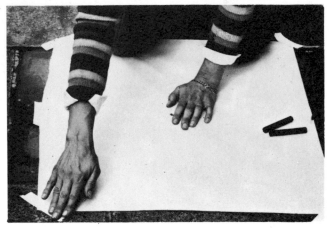

2. Lay your paper over the cover and stick or weight it down.

3. Rub the stick of colour gently but firmly over the whole area. (You may need a pad for your knees!) Go over any faint bits again before lifting your rubbing.

4. My doggy friend thought white on black paper was best.

RUBBINGS

Take rubbings of leaves and coins with wax crayon on thin paper. Mount or frame them nicely. See pages 108–111.

COLLECTING THINGS

You can make a collection out of almost anything from bus tickets to old motor car horns. It rather depends on the space available, and what sort of person you are.

If you like spending hours delving into history you may choose something like old newspapers. If you are a patient, clean and tidy person stamps are for you, and then a more slapdash character is better off with 'any old iron' – keys, locks, flat irons or old farm implements, for instance.

The most unusual collection I ever saw was one of **chimney pots** – but they are rather big for the average home.

Here are some ideas you may not have thought of for things which are fun to collect.

Badges from festivals, films, holiday resorts and clubs can take you over if you're not careful!

KEYS – A COLLECTION

Keys for trunks and cases, furniture and doors and windows.

The big ones on the left of the curved line are very old door keys. The straight ones at the other end of the line are for window locks. The details on keys are fascinating. This one is Canadian and has a 'fleur de lys' – a French symbol – on it. Why do you think that is?

One of these keys is not really a key – can you see which one and guess what it is? Answers on page 140.

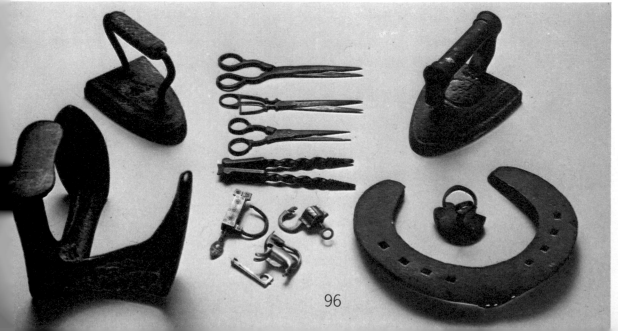

ANY OLD IRON

Scissors – irons – padlocks – horseshoes. These old padlocks come from Iran. The flat irons are from England – they used to heat up the flat irons on the kitchen range. Do you know what the strange thing bottom left is?

Answer on page 140.

TINS

Unusual tins, tubes and packets make a good collection. You can find lots of different ones for cough-sweets, ointments, polish, biscuits and so on.

MEDALS

THINGS FOR WRITING WITH

Most of these are fountain pens. The two marble-looking ones are the oldest – many old fountain pens have got **real gold** nibs which can be cleaned up and polished and often there is a rubber bladder inside for the ink – this has usually rotted and needs replacing.

The two top pens are ball-points. The fat one came from America and has ten colours.

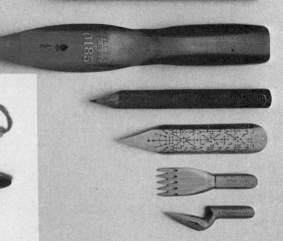

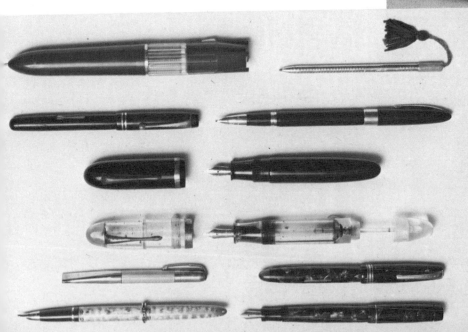

Here's a rare selection of pen nibs.

By the way, one of the pens on the left isn't for writing with – which one and what is it?

When was the first ball point produced?

Answers page 140.

SPOONS

Single spoons can form a beautiful collection. They don't have to be silver or silver plate. Get lots of different shapes, find out what they were used for – jam, coffee, sugar, salt and so on.

BOXES

Small boxes like these can cost quite a lot in junk and antique shops – but if you save up and buy them one by one your collection can become very valuable. If you are buying things, always get them in **good condition.**

MUGS

I have a friend who has collected mugs for years. She has 250 and these are some of them. They are all mugs commemorating British Jubilees and royal marriages and coronations. If you hold this one up to the light you can see through the bottom a transparent portrait of Queen Alexandra.

Do some detective work and find out more about your collection. You can look through old magazines and newspapers or in art galleries for early advertisements and pictures showing the things you have saved and discover the dates when people used them, what they were for and where they were made. Below are two old pictures showing smoothing irons in use.

 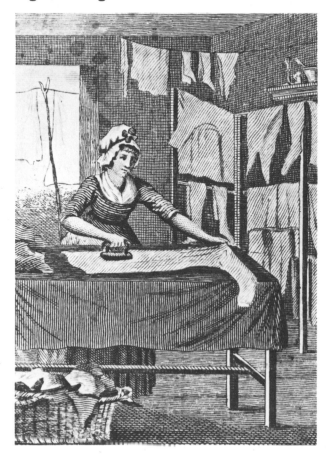

Display your collection nicely. Arrange things in interesting shapes. Try out different backgrounds:
Tins – on foil
Shells – on a tray of sand
Silver – on velvet
Medals – on natural hessian or bright red wool
I think these small glasses look best against black paper.

OPEN UP A DUSTBIN BAG...

...FOR DUSTBIN FASHION

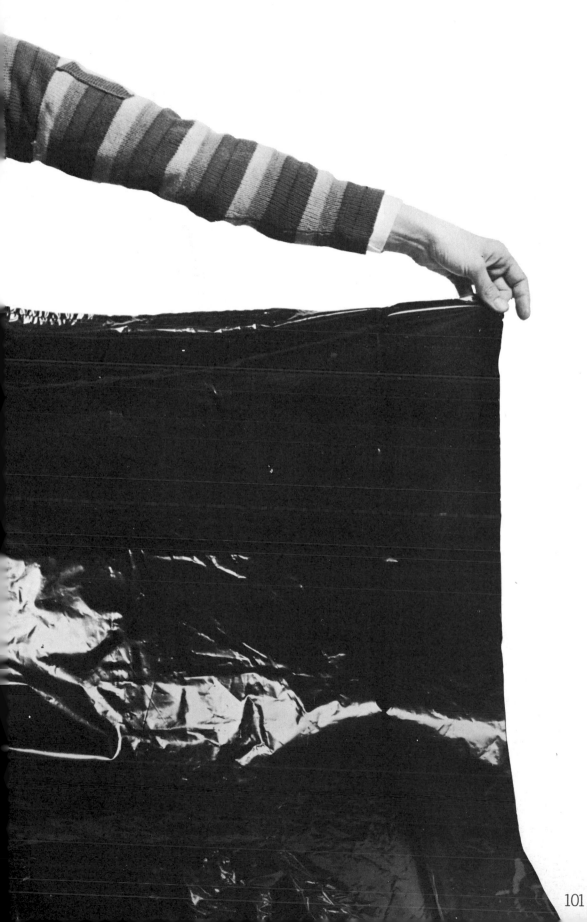

DUSTBIN FASHION

Try making clothes from a polythene dustbin-bag – a clean one! You can get different colours, but I like black.

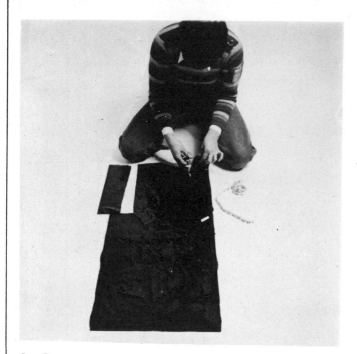

An Apron

1. Cut out an apron shape.

2. Check it for size.

3. Ties can be stapled, or tied on through small holes.

A Rain Poncho

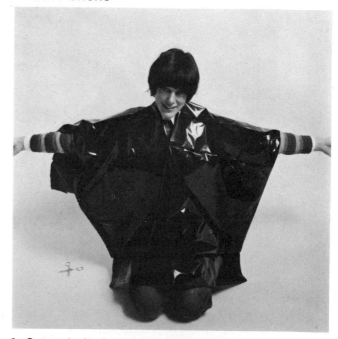

1. Cut a hole for your head in the middle of the open bag. Decorate it with flowers, stripes or a skull and cross bones. Tie or stick the sides. You need special glue to stick on polythene flowers and shapes.

DECORATE YOUR DEN

Have you got a room of your own? Or do you share one? Here are some easy cheap ideas to make it a bit different.

Planks and old bricks can make great shelves.
If you like, paint the bricks bright colours or even **gold.**

DECORATE YOUR DOOR

Use cut-out coloured paper to make a boring old door more interesting. Here are some ideas to inspire you – but think up your own. Stick in place with 'easy remove' tape or peel-off pads so you can have a change.

A SLEEPY CLOWN

A CROOKED FRONT DOOR

PEEK-A-BOO FLOWER

WINDOW BLINDS

Treat yourself to a new blind or window-hanging to cheer up a dull view. Make a mock stained-glass window with tissue-paper shapes on greaseproof paper or a real black-out job from a big black polythene bag.

PIRATE'S CABIN

SEE THRU' AND SUNNY

MOCK STAINED-GLASS

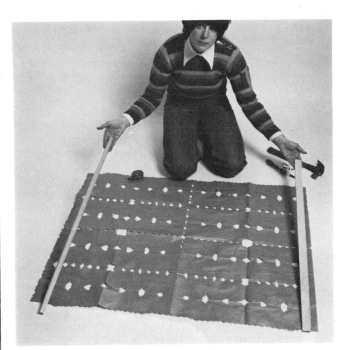

Screw two 'eyes' into your blind and hang up on two hooks (ask someone to screw them in the top of the window-frame for you). You can roll the blind up and loop it to the screws with string.

1. Fold up a big piece of brown parcel-paper several times and cut out patterns from it. (See page 37).

2. Using tough tape stick rods to the top and bottom. I used battening at the top and dowel (the rounded stuff) at the bottom.

FRAMING YOUR PICTURES

We often cut out pictures we like from papers and magazines – or draw and paint something worth keeping. But how often do they get shoved away in a drawer never to be seen again? Here are some ways to display your favourite pictures.

1. Take two sheets of card the same shape and size. Cut a hole – square, round or diamond-shaped – in one. Use a ruler to measure the size and position.

2. Tape the two pieces together on three sides. Tape the **front only** of the fourth side.

3. Stick a card strip as a stand on the back (or a loop of string to hang it up with).

4. Slide in your picture. My edges are a bit crooked because I didn't use a ruler. You can do better!

WALL BANNERS

Make a wall banner and stick a picture on it. This is a rubbing I took of an old coalhole cover in a London street.

PICTURE BLOCKS

Wood 'off-cuts' from builders or timber merchants are often interesting shapes, very cheap and can be used to back favourite pictures.

1. Sandpaper the rough edges. Stick the picture down well. Leave to dry flat, under heavy books.

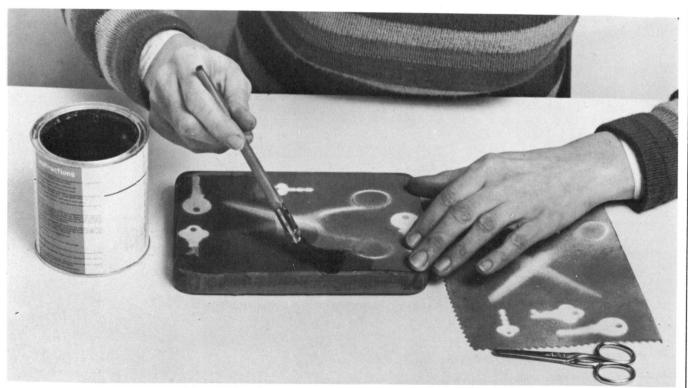

2. Paint the edges of the wood black (or a colour). Varnish with shiny clear varnish.

Screw a ring in the top or make a ribbon loop round the head of a screw.
(Make sure it is in the centre or it will hang crooked.)

Copies of famous pictures look lovely as picture blocks – so do old coins.

WALL BOARDS

Take a large sheet of heavy cardboard or hardboard or wood. Ask someone to cut it straight for you with a saw. Paint it, or cover it with printed paper or fabric and stick on different boxes and containers for holding things. Screw in hooks too. Maybe a mirror-tile, or a large note pad could be the centre of your board.

That's Peter, our photographer, in the mirror. Want to see more of him? Turn to page 141.

MYSTERY LOG

This is a wonderful recipe I learned from an American friend. No-one could guess what was in it. You need:

1 packet of ginger biscuits (round)
Fruit juice (I used tinned, and the fruit too) or mixed instant coffee
Cream
Grated chocolate

1. Soak each biscuit well in a shallow dish of juice or coffee (don't let them break up). Pile them on edge against each other to form a log and pour a little more juice over.

2. Whip the cream and spread all over the biscuits. Make it rough with a fork.

3. Finish off with grated chocolate or nuts — add fruit if you wish.
* This should be left in the fridge overnight.

112

CHOCOLATE GRAPES

Melt some chocolate squares together with a little water in a bowl inside a container filled with hot water. Dip grapes on cocktail sticks into the mixture, put on foil and set in fridge. Delicious!

* Chocolate apples and mandarin segments are good too.

Pack some in a box for a glamorous present. See page 134.

SUPERFLAN

You need:
Flan or sponge (bought)
Tinned fruit (whatever you like)
Cream

1. Fill flan with fruit – make a pretty pattern. Pour on a little juice to keep it moist.

2. Whip the cream until it stands in peaks. Dollop (or pipe) into place and sprinkle with nuts, raisins or glacé cherries.

Don't forget to **wash up** – and while we're on the subject of **dish cloths** turn over!

DISH CLOTH VEST

1. Buy two identical dish cloths – make sure they will stretch right across you with room to spare.

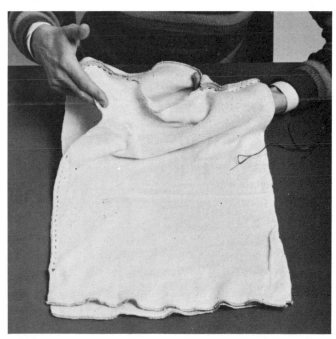

2. Sew across the shoulders and down the sides – leave plenty of room for head and arms.

You can try with safety pins first to see how big the gaps should be.

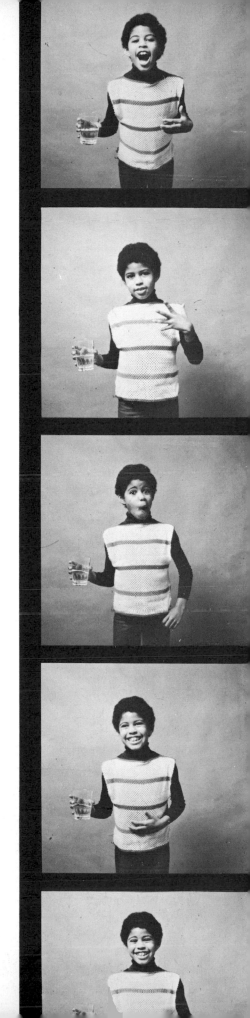

STRING ALONG

This is called macramé.

Learn this simple knot first. Take two very long strands of string. Fold them in half to make four, tie a loop and put it round a firm nail or the leg of a chair.

1. Work only with the two outside strands. Take the right across in front of the middle two and behind the left strand.

2. Push the left around behind the middle two and into the right loop.

3. Pull the whole strand through the loop.

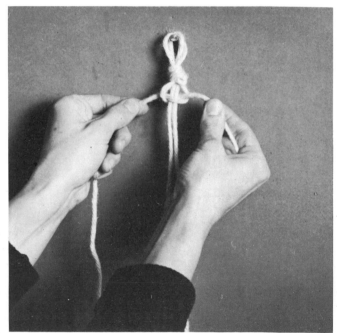

4. Tighten and there's your first knot.

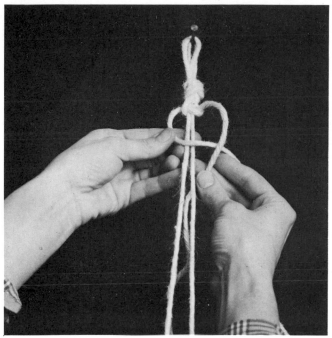

5. Now do the same starting with the left strand – this is called a flat knot. Soon you will be on the way to making a **belt!**

For the **twisting knot** just keep starting with the same hand instead of changing each time. I added glass beads to mine as I went.

NOW try a **plant holder** – start with three lots of four strands.

STRING ALONG

Make other things out of string too.

Buy, or better still, save natural and coloured string – or dye it with cold water dye or coloured ink.

This pendant and napkin ring were made by winding string round and round on cardboard (a disc or a roll). Mats take longer but look good too. Start from the outside edge. Try changing colours as you go. Stick with glue.

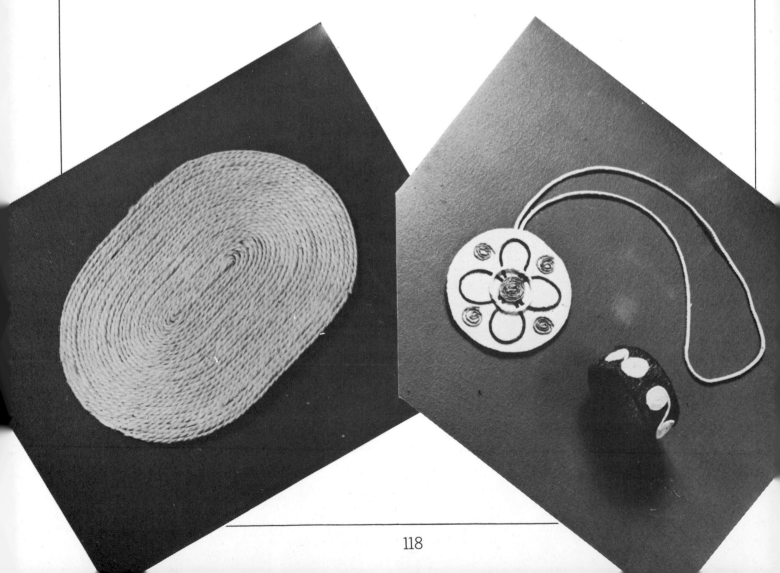

A SSSSSNAKE

1. Cut out a circle of paper or thin card.

2. Draw a snake on it like this. It seems easier if you start from the outside, tail first. Colour him brightly.

3. Cut out your snake tail first. It takes ages! For goodness sake don't cut off his head.

4. Thread cotton through his head and hang him up.

* Bigger ones make unusual mats for a party.

POM-POM SCARF

We made this super scarf from a roll of cotton stockinette 'scrim' (stuff for wrapping meat in and cleaning cars), cheap from hardware and household stores or a garage. Sew matching pom-poms on the ends. See page 8.

You can **dye** your stockinette first with cold water dye if you want. See page 74.

120

COLLARS AND TIES

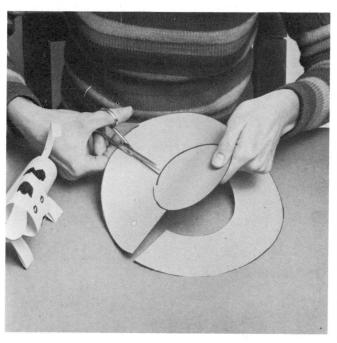

1. Draw a smaller circle (approximately 9 inches or 22 centimetres across) inside a big circle (13 inches or 32 centimetres across). Keep it in the middle.

2. Now cut out the small circle plus a section of the big circle (a sort of wide 'key hole' shape).

3. Decorate your collar. I used a cut-up paper doily which looked like lace – but you can use buttons, sequins, paint or stickers. Tie on your collars with tapes fastened to each end. You can make a tie too if you like and pin it on under a plain collar.

EGYPTIANS

Jason did a project on Ancient Egypt and he thought he would like to dress up as an Egyptian Prince.

We made this simple cheap outfit from an old sheet and a collar based on the one on page 121. Take two wide strips of old sheet (or any other suitable fabric). Measure them against yourself for width and length – you are always wider than you think!

Tie two knots on the shoulders and tie rope or a belt round your waist. Cut out fabric collar. Make a paper pattern first. Decorate with any of these:

Pasta
Dried beans
Sequins, beads
Jewels
Buttons
Curtain rings
Wool and string
Glitter

We used pull rings from drink-cans too. We cut a longer tunic, the same shape, for Sadie. Their sandals are just criss-crossed football laces.

Sadie found the hessian rather scratchy, but you could use cotton or felt instead.

ROMAN BULLA

In Ancient Rome young Roman boys used to wear medallions called **Bullas** which denoted their manhood – you can make some with foil, string and card.

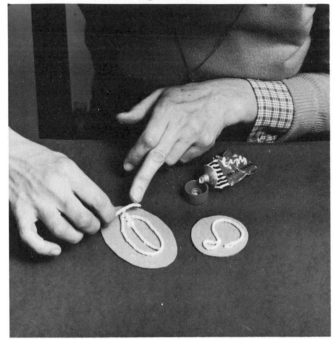

1. Cut out small rounds of card. Glue on string in interesting shapes.

2. Cover with foil, pressing down well (glue in places). Make a hole in the top with a sharp pencil – hang on ribbon or wool.

A CLAY BOWL

In the old days, before factories, people used to make their own bowls for drinking and eating out of. This is one method they used called the 'coil' method.

Make a long, even roll of modelling clay (or plasticine) and, starting at the base, curl it round and round and up and up. When the bowl is as big as you want, wet your fingers and press all the joins into one another.

New clay – set it with hardener following the instructions.
Ordinary clay – get it fired by someone who has a kiln.

THINGS TO DO WITH YOUR FRIENDS

HOW THEY WERE

Take different times in the past and find out what you can of the lives of the people – how they lived, dressed, worked, ate.

Visit museums
Cut out pictures
Make wall charts
Dress up
Write and act short scenes or even a play set in the time you've chosen.

You could start with the Ancient Egyptians. Each person could make a collar. Or a 'coil' clay bowl.

TRANSPORT

Study various types of transport, each person taking a different method – Air, Road, Rail, Sea.

Compare speeds – efficiency – history and development.
Collect pictures – licence numbers – advertisements from papers and magazines.
Visit museums and depots. Organize a trip round a big car factory or an airport with a grown-up.

FOOD

Make a study of the different kinds of food.

Chinese
Indian
Cowboy
Eskimo, etc.

Visit a big canteen or factory kitchen with a grown-up.
Make wall charts.
Discover the protein and vitamin values in food – what makes you fat or thin – what gives you energy?

Enjoy a Chinese or Indian meal for a change – eat with chop-sticks; you can often buy them very cheaply and it's great fun.

ANIMAL CORNER

Get together at school and ask to have an animal corner.
Make sure everyone in the group can be relied on to do their share of feeding and cleaning and exercise.
Watch the different habits of the creatures.
Mate and breed from them if you are allowed, and have space.

Rabbits
Hamsters
Gerbils
Guinea pigs
Chickens
Mice
Lizards
Fish
Tortoises

You can arrange for chosen people to take them home in the holidays.

GROW SOMETHING

Lots of bulbs in pretty bowls and single ones in mugs
make nice presents. Plant them early enough for the
shoots to have started before you give them away
and don't forget to water them. You can keep them in the
dark at first; it helps them grow.

Sometimes fruit pips – oranges, lemons, grapes and
so on – will grow too, but don't forget to label yours. I
forgot and I cannot remember what these in the
white mug were now – melon, I think!

Make special gift tags for your 'growing presents'.

Try conkers and avocado pear stones too. Some
people put them over a jar of water and put them in earth
when the roots and shoots have started –
but I just stick them straight in the earth
and look how lucky I have
been. Those above are avocado pear trees.

Chop off carrot tops and stand them in a shallow
saucer of water – they will start to grow new, green,
feathery leaves.

SMALL ANIMALS

Are you thinking of keeping a pet? If so – think first about all the lonely, hungry, miserable and sick animals which began life as pampered, cared-for friends.

Now look at this sad picture of a dog which was just chucked out on a motor way and left to starve.

If the R.S.P.C.A. hadn't rescued him in time he would have died. The same happens to thousands of domestic pets every year.

Now, if you are still determined to have a pet, decide:

1. What kind would be suitable for your home and family. (Does your father like dogs? Is your sister scared of mice?)

2. If you are sick or away others will have to care for it. So, do your neighbours and friends like pets?

3. Think of the pet's needs and your own life style – time available for walks, company and so on.

4. Are there other animals in the house already? Think of them too. It's only fair.

5. Space – have you a garden or a park nearby?

6. Money – can you afford to provide for the pet you want? It will need a house, cage or basket – food and drink – vet and medicine when sick – brushing and grooming things.

When you think you know what you want, buy or borrow a reliable booklet about that kind of animal just to see if you could manage to provide the things it will need. Then you are ready to welcome the new friend into your life.

Even the smallest animals need love and care, here's Candy with her mouse, **Smartie Artie.** He is one of a long list of small animals she has in her family. Smartie Artie is so-called because he escapes a lot!

Try this quiz to find out how much you know about domestic pets.

1. Dutch, Himalayan, Polish, Lap are four kinds of what?

2. Should a rabbit be given salt? Yes or no?

3. Should a rabbit eat little lettuce? Lots of lettuce? None at all?

4. Rabbits and tortoises should be kept apart. True or false?

5. The natural lifespan of a tortoise is one year? Twenty years? A hundred years?

6. When should you buy your tortoise? Before or after July?

7. When buying a tortoise it should measure more than 10 centimetres across the shell underneath – why?

8. You can tell the sex of a tortoise by its tail – true or false?

9. How long does it take for a mated bitch to have puppies?

10. How many meals a day should a puppy have just after weaning?

11. How can you tell if a dog has worms?

12. Is it better to train your dog when it is (a) excited or (b) quiet?

13. How old should a female cat be before she can be spayed (to stop her having kittens)?

14. Infectious Enteritis is a deadly disease for cats. Is it true that if a cat survives the disease it can never get it again?

15. You should always put your cat out at night – true or false?

16. At what age can kittens be taken from their mother?

17. What is a gerbil?

18. Is it true that hamsters are short-sighted?

19. Male guinea pigs should be kept apart – true or false?

20. You can tell the sex of a budgie by its beak – true or false?

Answers to quiz on page 140.

EATING OUTDOORS

Barbecues Ask a grown up first – choose a sheltered spot, not too near overhanging foliage.

1. Place two bricks on each end of a sheet of kitchen foil. Add barbecue fire-lighters and a small pile of charcoal on top.

2. Ask a grown up to light the fire. When the charcoal turns white add a bit more. When it is all white add a wire-grill rack and start cooking. (For hotter cooking lay the bricks flat.)

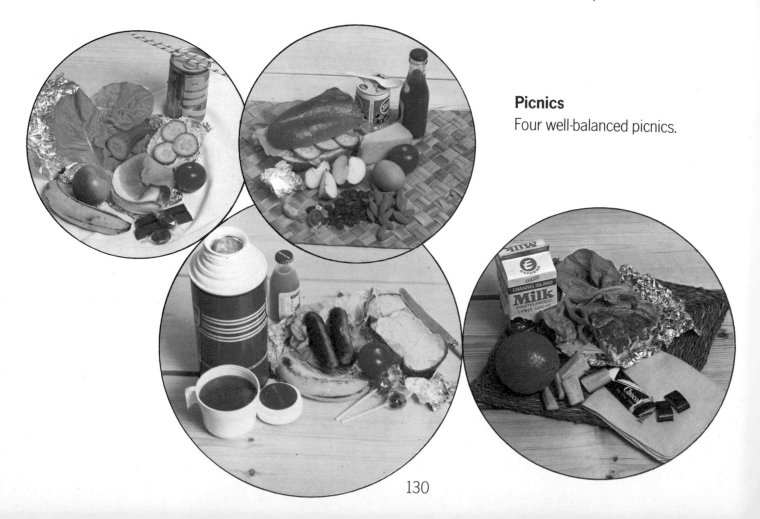

Picnics

Four well-balanced picnics.

PICNICS

I love picnics – food always tastes much nicer out of doors, don't you think? Winter picnics are fun too but do wrap up warm.

Remember – take warm clothes, the right shoes – bathing things and towel if you swim.

Good picnics should include each of these:
1. Meat, fish, cheese or eggs
2. Bread, rolls, biscuits
3. Salad and fruit
4. Sweet things
5. Drink (and extra water)

Smudge says – dogs can't drink from small cans and don't like fizzy drinks!

Always remember fresh water and a bowl for your dog.

Always take away your rubbish.

Always shut gates and respect other people's property.

TRAVELLING ON

When you have to travel anywhere in a car, bus or train, don't just sit there like a bored lemon or fidget and wriggle about like a worm with fleas driving everyone else bonkers –

Look around you…

Have fun – play some games.

Here are a few useful tips and some games to play if you are on the move.

Longer trips need more planning, of course, but the basic problems always apply on a journey.

1. You may get hungry or thirsty.

2. You may get cold or hot.

3. You may want the lavatory or even feel sick.

4. You may leave something behind or lose your ticket, or even lose your way.

Make up a small food pack the night before – see page 130.

Dress sensibly with an extra layer (jumper or cardigan) that can be added or taken off – trains and buses can be hot and stations cold.

Use the lavatory before you leave home and notice where the public ones are on stations, in trains and garages, just in case.

Prone to travel sickness? Beastly isn't it? Don't eat a huge sickly meal just before your journey. I find something like cereal and milk or plain or digestive biscuits pretty reliable. Don't ever read or write in a bus or car.

Check your belongings before you leave and at each change of transport and **on arriving**.

Make sure you know the **exact address** of where you are going and where you have come from, and **telephone numbers** too if any, and be sure you are on the right train or bus.

I have been lost several times so I know!…

Once I got into the wrong end of a train which split in half and went in two different directions – my half took me miles out of my way – I felt so stupid and quite scared, but I managed to telephone home and found out the next train, arriving very late, very tired and starving hungry.

Some good travelling games:

NUMBERS

Quickly add up the numbers on each number-plate on cars, buses, and motor-bikes – if they make an odd number you score one point, if even two points.

For example:

756 = 18
  1 + 8 = 9 score 1
551 = 11
  1 + 1 = 2 score 2
811 = 10
  1 + 0 = 1 score 1
774 = 18
  1 + 8 = 9 score 1

RHYME TIME

One person starts a rhyme and the others follow in turn.

Here's an example:

Ben: I walked along the lane **alone**
Susan: And there I met an aged **crone**
Alison: She asked where there was a tele**phone**
Ben: I found it underneath a **stone!**

You see – the end words rhyme.

You can make up longer rhymes if there are more people. Try using simple words at the end of each line which have lots of rhymes to them:

pen	rain	allow	shore	cat	bait
men	pain	bow	more	mat	plate
den	stain	cow	core	sat	mate
hen	main	how	door	hat	gate
ten	wane	row	lore	fat	eight
	Dane	now	four	flat	ate
		sow		plait	hate
		vow			date

Spot: an unusual lamp post.   **Spot:** a postbox in a wall.   **Spot spot:** twin telephone kiosks.

SPOT

Make a list of things worth points according to how often they are seen and the type of journey you are taking.

For example:
telephone box = 2
postbox = 2
parked motor-bike = 1

policeman = 1
dog = 1
Rolls-Royce = 5

telegraph pole = 2
cows = 1
sheep = 1
goods train = 5

Each time someone sees something on the list, point and shout **"spot"** and if they get in first, they score the right number of points – most points wins.

COUNTRIES, RIVERS, TOWNS AND SEAS

One player names a country (or it can be a town, mountain, sea, river or lake). Let's say FRANCE. The next player has to follow with one beginning with the last letter of the first name – ENGLAND.

A typical list might be:

France – England – Denmark – Korea – Andes (mountains) – Sardinia – Asia (continent) and so on.

There seem to be lots of As. See what you think.

Have a good trip!

Why not make a **map** of your route before you leave home?

BOXES

Ever tried to make a box? – it's simple, and once learned never forgotten. Here's how.

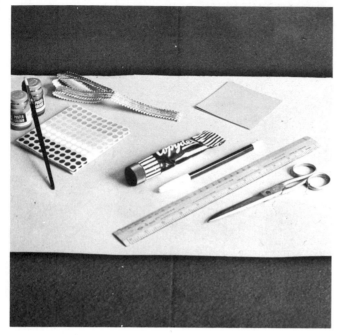

1. You need something exactly square to draw round – make a small piece of paper square, see page 68. Stick it to card and cut it out.
Take a large sheet of paper...

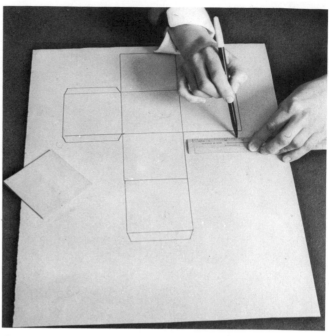

2. Draw round your square six times to form this cross-shape. Use your ruler to draw tabs top and bottom of the side squares and one on the long end (which will become the lid).

3. Cut it out – don't cut off the flaps!

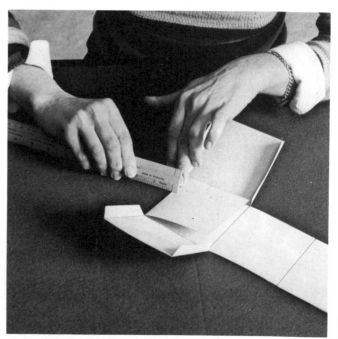

4. Fold towards you along all the lines; a ruler helps you get really sharp creases.

5. Fold in the flaps too.

6. Glue the four side tabs and stick them inside to form corners.

7. Decorate as you like. I used paper butterflies
   sequins and glitter
   braid and lace
   paint ,leaves and flowers etc.

8. Make them any size, using thicker cardboard if they are big.

P.S. You can make a smashing set of building bricks for a younger child. Stick the lid down and decorate with the alphabet or animals.

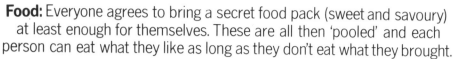

CHEAP PARTIES: SWOP SHOP PARTY

Everyone likes parties, but they are often a bit expensive – here are two ideas that are almost cheaper than staying at home!

Food: Everyone agrees to bring a secret food pack (sweet and savoury) at least enough for themselves. These are all then 'pooled' and each person can eat what they like as long as they don't eat what they brought.

Drink: The one giving the party should provide the drinks and plates etc., or you can tell your guests to bring these too if you are feeling really poor and lazy. But remember, some people don't like fizzy drinks so do have some fruit squash handy.

What you do

Tell the guests to look out all the things they are fed up with. Keep the value low. Ask a grown-up to help make up a table as a rough guide. For example:

Best = 50 swop points
Good = 40 swop points
Fair = 30 swop points
Poor = 20 swop points
Rubbish = 10 swop points

Mark things clearly with their swop value, and forget money altogether.

Each person arrives with their selection in a big bag. Someone acts as Chief Merchant to sort out any bargaining and places them in piles according to their swop value.

Then the swopping begins.

You can make direct swops – a 20 swop point for a 20 swop point or exchange a 20 swop point for two 10 swop points and so on.

Anything left goes back to the owner unless he feels he can reduce the swop value to make it a better deal.

Important: You must ask permission before swopping things – it is so embarrassing for you if you have to ask for something back.

And don't forget to take everything away with you, or whoever gave the party can charge 1p a day fine for each uncollected swop. These funds go towards the next party.

What kind of…?

A swop game

A player stands in the middle and imagines to be someone else in the room. The others ask questions.
'If you were an animal what kind would you be?'
'If you were a car what kind would you be?'
If you were a flower
television programme
item of clothing
person in history
time of day, etc.
The first one to guess who the player is gets the next turn.

✄ CHEAP PARTIES: TRAMPS' PARTY ✄
Everyone dresses up in old torn clothes and hats like a tramp.

Food: Door-step sandwiches
Fish and chips
Bangers and mash
Baked potatoes with grated cheese
Raw tomatoes
Jam tarts

All or any of those eaten from grease-proof bags wrapped in thick newspaper.

Drink: Any you want, but it should be tea out of tin mugs!

Decorations: Make 'em yourself from newspaper.

Games: Have a 'treasure hunt' – wrap the 'treasure' in newspaper,
hide it and lay a trail to it with newspaper.

Pass the Parcel is an old favourite and a good game for a newspaper party.
Wrap up a small, exciting present – sweets, a hand-made string pendant,
a small plaster object, a badge, a nice old tin or spoon for instance.

Then wrap it up again and again ten or twelve times with newspaper and string or
ribbon. The players sit in a ring. When the music starts each one passes the parcel
from one hand across to the other, then to the next person (keep in rhythm if you can).

Whoever has the parcel when the music stops starts to unwrap it as fast as they can –
but the music starts again soon and they have to pass it on.

Whoever has the parcel when the last wrapping is completely off keeps the present.

Important: Whoever plays the music should not look at the group so there is no
favouritism!

For a really hard game make them undo the string, not tear it off. How they'll hate you!

Old Tom This is a variation of 'My aunt went to market', a special one for tramps…

Guest A Old Tom went to the junkheap and he found: A rusty tin of boot polish…
Guest B Old Tom went to the junkheap and he found: A rusty tin of boot polish and a spare tyre…
Guest C Old Tom went to the junkheap and he found: A rusty tin of boot polish, a spare tyre, and a broken gold watch…

Each guest follows on, adding another item, until someone forgets one and has to
drop out…last in is the winner.

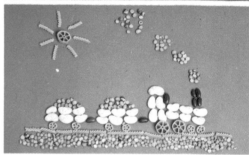

COLLAGE

A collage or a montage is a picture made up of bits and pieces. A bit like picture sculpture. Try some of these.

Fabrics
Cardboard boxes
Dried beans, peas, pasta
Eggshells, nutshells
Nuts and bolts and paperclips
Stones and shells
Leaves and flowers
Buttons and beads
Wool and string

You can make an abstract picture, or one which represents something—an animal or a scene perhaps. Consider your materials first and don't always go for the obvious. Fur and feathers for a cat is nice, but nuts and bolts can be surprisingly effective too.

ANSWER TIME

Did you answer these questions?

Page 21 Smudge appears 14 times in this book if you count the cover!

Page 54 Rubbing the film creates static electricity.

Page 54 Tines. At first forks had only two tines. The four tined fork became usual at the end of the 1700s.

Page 74 A = 4
B = 7
C = 2
D = 1
E = 6
F = 3
G = 5

Page 96 The French settled in Canada in the early 1500s and have been there ever since.

Page 96 The third one from the right in row three is a lighter.

Page 96 A cobbler's last for mending shoes on.

Page 97 The second one up from the bottom on the left is a propelling knife.

Page 97 The 1930s. The first ball point pen was produced in 1938 and widely used by 1944.

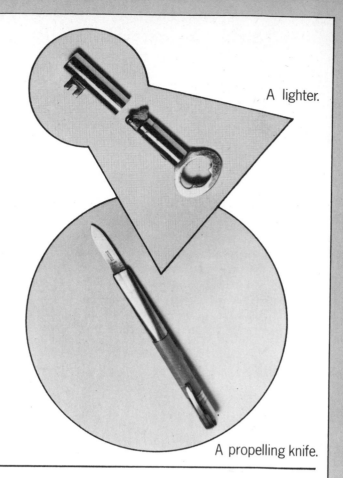

A lighter.

A propelling knife.

Answers to Animal Quiz on page 129

1. These are four kinds of rabbit.

2. Yes, rock-salt, and a mineral lick should be freely available in the rabbit's hutch.

3. A rabbit should only have very little lettuce (it contains Laudanum, which is a poison).

4. False – often a rabbit and a tortoise (or chickens or a guinea pig) can strike up a friendly relationship, but be more careful about cats and dogs!

5. Healthy tortoises have been known to live for over a hundred years, but unfortunately, because of the dreadful conditions they suffer when being transported for sale, many die within one year.

6. Before July, if you live in a cold climate to give it time to adjust before the winter.

7. A well grown tortoise has a better chance of survival. Also look for bright eyes and a clean, active body.

8. True – the male has a long tapering tail, the female a short stumpy one.

9. Nine weeks from when she is mated.

10. After weaning, normally 5-7 weeks of age, puppies should have four meals a day at first, usually of cereals, baked brown bread, puppy meal, milk, meat, etc.

11. Loss of weight and condition, dull coat and a swollen tummy can indicate worms, but it can mean other things too – always consult a vet if in doubt.

12. It is always better to train a dog when it is quiet.

13. Have a female kitten spayed after four or five months – a male kitten can be neutered at the same age.

14. Yes, it becomes immune – but Infectious Enteritis is usually deadly. Vomiting, faint crying and blood stained motions and loss of appetite are indications of the disease. You can have your cat vaccinated against it.

15. False – you should never turn out an unwilling cat at night. Some **prefer** to stay out. Town cats should be kept in after dark with access to a litter tray.

16. Kittens should be left with their mother until they are eight weeks old.

17. A gerbil is a desert rat. It is a rodent, but is not as smelly as mice and rats and makes an excellent pet.

18. Yes – Hamsters are nocturnal, and short-sighted. Never put your hamster where it may fall, as they have delicate bones and can injure themselves easily.

19. True – adult male guinea pigs should be kept apart as they are inclined to fight. This happens with other male animals too, so always take care.

20. True – really it is the horny bit above the beak. In the male it is blue, in the female brown.

Score one point for each correct answer.
1-5 poor, 5-10 average, 10-15 good, 15-20 excellent.

You saw a bit of him on Page 111.Here he is!
Peter Tebbitt who took nearly all the photographs,
with **Smudge,** our mascot.

Thank you to all the friends who helped with this book,
especially those who made some of the lovely finished
things to show in the pictures:

Ray Child
Danielle Sacher
Eileen Geipel
Jimmy Tucker

And to the following, who provided extra material
and advice:

E. J. Arnold and Sons
Copydex Limited
Dylon International
Royal Society for the Prevention of Cruelty to Animals

Educational Advisor: Claire Chappell, B.ed.
Extra photography:
Barry Breckon
Tony Hutchings
The Radio Times Hulton Picture Library

My bright, striped sweater made by Knutz.